Consistency and Credibility?

Environmental Reporting, Environmental Performance
Indicators and Economic Performance

von

Marcus Wagner

Tectum Verlag
Marburg 2005

Wagner, Marcus:
Consistency and Credibility?.
Environmental Reporting, Environmental Performance
Indicators and Economic Performance.
/ von Marcus Wagner
- Marburg : Tectum Verlag, 2005
ISBN 978-3-8288-8646-9

© Tectum Verlag

Tectum Verlag
Marburg 2005

TABLE OF CONTENTS

Acknowledgements

I would like to thank Professor Stefan Schaltegger, head of the Centre for Sustainability Management (CSM) at the University of Lüneburg, for his time and thoughts, for accepting me as a Habilitation candidate and for enabling the continuity of my work at CSM.

Dr. Christopher Cohrs (University of Erlangen-Nürnberg) was available for discussions on statistical aspects, made critical and valuable comments on my work and always was a good friend to me. I would like to thank all of my colleagues, friends and relatives for their patience and understanding during the period of writing this book and especially Imad Mahayri M.Phil. who was not only a good friend, but also always very supportive of my endeavours.

Finally, I wish to express my sincere thanks to all those companies who provided environmental reports and additional data and in doing so made possible this analysis. Knowing that it is not their primary purpose I am grateful that staff in these firms took the time and trouble to respond to the surveys that form the empirical basis of the work presented in this book. I hope they will be able to benefit from the results of my research. The form and content of this work and any errors remaining are the sole responsibility of the author.

Last, in no way least, but instead very personally I would like to thank my wife Theodora and my parents for their continuous love and support. You made it all possible and I owe you so much more than words can say. I wish to dedicate this book to them, and to my grandparents, Anneliese and Willi Alfred Herbert August Ebbecke, and Josef and Luise Wagner who in two centuries experienced both, sustainability (but also sometimes hardship) of country life as well as cruel unsustainability of war.

This book is dedicated to those most dear to me:
To Dora, my parents and my grandparents in deep gratefulness.

The objective of this book is to identify the extent of correlation between actual environmental performance, the use of physical environmental performance indicators (EPIs) and corporate environmental reporting in the paper and electricity industries in Germany and the UK and based on this to assess the relationship between environmental and economic performance. After reviewing the literature on environmental performance indicators, environmental performance measurement, environmental reporting and corporate environmental reports the book focuses in its first part on an analysis between actual environmental performance, the use of physical EPIs and the quality of corporate environmental reports (CERs) in the and paper and electricity industries. This analysis is based on a cross-sectional survey of CERs and an intersection of the environmental performance indicators used in the environmental reports allowing for comparison between sectors and countries. The results from the content analysis of the CERs and from computing quantitative EPIs were then combined in a statistical analysis. Using different statistical methods it identified possible correlation and patterns. The results suggest environmental performance is mainly country-related, possibly due to differences in environmental legislation. On the other hand, environmental reporting quality is predominantly linked to industry sectors.

The findings also imply, that the use of a higher number of indicators or the production of an elaborate environmental report does likely link in any strong fashion to the environmental performance of a company. However it seems that a detailed data collection process (e.g. supported by the use of an Eco-balance) and the resulting sound base data assist much the identification of optimisation potentials for improving environmental performance. Overall, this study indicates that consistency in environmental performance, use of EPIs and environmental reporting is rare. This implies that any assessment of the relationship between environmental and economic performance of firms needs to be based on actual environmental performance data and cannot take reporting quality or information about the intensity of use of specific tools, such as environmental performance indicators as a proxy variable.

Based on this finding, the second part of the book therefore analyses the relationship between environmental and economic performance and the influence of corporate environmental strategies. After formulating a theoretical model, results are reported from an empirical analysis of the two above industries (paper and electricity) for an enlarged data set covering four EU countries. It uses new data to test hypotheses derived from the theoretical model. For an emissions-based index in the paper industry, a predominantly negative relationship is found, whereas for an inputs-based index in the same industry no significant link is found. From the results it is concluded that for firms in the paper industry, oriented towards pollution prevention, the relationship between environmental and economic performance is better, however not significantly positive, but, as it seems in the best case insignificant. In the European electricity supply industry, the empirical analysis, for an emissions-based index of environmental performance, no significant relationship is found for electricity generators in the four European countries. Based on the results, the book's second part concludes that for firms in environmentally-intensive industries it is difficult to create a positive link between their environmental and economic performance, and that market settings (i.e. external factors) as well as strategy considerations (i.e. internal factors) both can have an effect, but situational aspects determine which of these dominates.

LIST OF FIGURES

LIST OF TABLES

XV

XVII

ACCA	Association of Chartered Certified Accountants
AIChE	American Institute of Chemical Engineers
ANOVA	Analysis of Variance
AOX	Adsorbable Organic Halogens
BImSchG	Bundesimmissionsschutzgesetz
BITE	Business in the Environment
BOD	Biological Oxygen Demand
CBA	Cost-Benefit Analysis
CER	Corporate Environmental Report
CERES	Coalition for Environmentally Responsible Economies
CO	Carbon Monoxide
CO_2	Carbon Dioxide
COD	Chemical Oxygen Demand
CRI	Chemicals Release Inventory
DIN	Deutsches Institut für Normung (German Institute for Standardisation)
EC	European Community
EEA	European Environment Agency
EER	Electronic Environmental Reporting
EMAS	EC Eco-Management and Audit Scheme
EPI	Environmental Performance Indicator
EPM	Environmental Performance Measurement

ER-I	Emissierregistratie-Industrie (Dutch Federal Emissions Inventory)
EVF	Environmental Value Fund
IÖW	Institut für ökologische Wirtschaftsforschung
IRRC	Investor Responsibility Research Center
ISO	International Standards Organisation
LCA	Life-Cycle Assessment / Life-Cycle Analysis
MWh	Megawatt hours
N	Nitrogen
NACE	European Standard Industrial Classification
NO_x	Nitrogenous Oxides
NRTEE	National Round Table on the Environment and the Economy
P	Phosphor, phosphorous
pH	Potential of hydrogen (measure of acidity or alkalinity of a liquid)
R	Pearson correlation coefficient
Rpb	Coefficient for point-biserial correlation
SETAC	Society of Environmental Toxicology and Chemistry
SO_2	Sulphur Dioxide
TQM	Total Quality Management
TSS	Total Suspended Solids
UNEP	United Nations Environment Programme
WBCSD	World Business Council for Sustainable Development

| WICE | World Industry Council for the Environment |
| WRI | World Resources Institute |

1. Introduction

1.1 Objective and Approach of the Book

This book consists of two fairly distinct parts which are however linked by the underlying data as well as a two-stage approach to an overarching research theme.

The objective of the first section of this book is to identify the extent of correlation between the physical environmental performance of a company, the use of quantitative physical environmental performance indicators[1] and the quality of a company's corporate environmental reporting in two industrial sectors in two EU countries. The industrial sectors chosen for this analysis are the pulp and paper industry and the electricity supply and generation industry[2]. The countries in which firms in these sectors are analysed with regard to the above objective are the United Kingdom and Germany[3]. In the analysis, the physical environmental performance of a company is defined by its performance with regard to environmental aspects throughout the book[4].

---

[1] The term 'environmental performance indicator(s)' is in the following usually abbreviated as EPI.

[2] The sector classification is based on NACE codes i.e. NACE 21.1 (Paper) and NACE 40.1 (Electricity).

[3] The two sectors and countries were chosen since a high number of companies produce environmental reports or site-level environmental statements under EMAS in these two sectors and countries. These are usually externally validated and therefore guarantee a sufficient level of data quality. Additionally both sectors produce fairly homogenous products, which makes a comparison of physical environmental performance possible. In the second section of the book, the Netherlands and Italy are additionally included.

[4] Next to the term 'environmental aspect' the terms environmental pressure, stressor, environmental intervention, loading and environmental burden are also used synonymously in the literature.

An environmental aspect is defined as an "element of an organisation's activities, products or services that can interact with the environment" (DIN, 1995). Physical environmental performance indicators (EPIs) are one way to describe environmental aspects and consequently physical environmental performance. Such physical indicators describe mass, energy or pollutant flows through the manufacturing process (e.g. the use of energy or water resources or the emissions of pollutants from processes or products) which constitute a direct relationship between firms and the environment. Physical EPIs can be quantitative (i.e. measured on a continuous, interval or ordinal scale) or qualitative (i.e. measured on a nominal scale).

The quantification of mass, energy and pollutant flows through the system boundary between a firm and the environment describes with high precision the environmental aspects of a firm and consequently permits precise and detailed statements about the physical environmental performance of a firm. Therefore for the book this approach has been chosen to analyse, in a first step, the reported physical environmental performance of companies in two industrial sectors (electricity and pulp and paper) in two countries (the United Kingdom and Germany).

In a second step, the actual physical environmental performance of companies in these two sectors, characterised on the basis of quantitative indicators describing mass, energy and pollutant flows is then compared with the use of such indicators in the companies' environmental reporting and the quality of such reporting in general. This is done by way of an in-depth statistical analysis using different methods in order to identify possible linkage (and its extent) between the variables used to describe actual physical environmental performance, use of quantitative

2

physical environmental performance indicators and the quality of the company's environmental reporting in general.

Also the statistical analysis seeks to identify general patterns in the data in order to interpret correctly the identified correlation. The data basis for the analysis is derived from a cross-sectional survey of the two sectors and countries based on the published environmental reports of companies in the relevant sectors in both countries[5]. These environmental reports are analysed by way of a content analysis, which uses accepted environmental benchmarking categories. These include general categories describing the quality of environmental reports. However, emphasis was placed on categories describing the use of quantitative indicators, the use of data collection and presentation methods that allow the use of such indicators, and categories that relate to the concept of sustainability.

The evaluation of the physical environmental performance of companies is based on a sub-set of quantitative physical environmental performance indicators used in the environmental reports. This allows for intra-industry as well as inter-industry comparison. The indicators used for evaluating actual environmental performance are also linked into the categories applied to assess the level of use of quantitative physical indi-

---

[5]   This of course introduces a bias as it is likely that companies that produce environmental reports are more concerned about environmental issues and should therefore express higher environmental performance levels than the industry average. However this is not of particular relevance for the scope of this study as it does not affect the relationship between the quality of environmental reporting and the quality of environmental performance. The reason for this is that this relationship can only be measured for the case that a company produces an environmental report and that therefore (a) it is unavoidable and (b) such bias would not obstruct analysing the questions that are at the core of this book which concern relationships.

cators in the environmental reports of the companies. Both variable sets gathered from the primary data in environmental reports are then analysed statistically as described above, using SPSS® and STATA®.

From this analysis, in a third step, several general and more specific hypotheses and research questions are addressed. Of general interest is, first of all, if comparability within and between sectors is possible at all or if comparison proves to be difficult even for such homogenous sectors with high data availability and quality as the two addressed in this study.

Where comparisons yield interpretable results, the question of immediate interest is, to what extent the level of environmental performance and the quality of environmental reports are consistent and consequently what credibility should be attributed to such reports. To answer these general questions correctly, several more specific hypotheses have to be tested that provide a more precise description of variations in the underlying data set. These include e.g. the effects of industry sector and country membership, influences of country-specific environmental legislation and approaches to environmental management and possible sector or national differences in the use of physical indicators and the quality of environmental reports.

1.2 The Structure of the Book and its Relation to Objective and Approach of the Book

To achieve the objectives stated and detailed above, the book is structured as follows: Following this introductory Chapter 1 the next three chapters review the in Chapter 2 relevant physical environmental performance indicators (EPIs), in Chapter 3 on the overall performance measurement system, and in Chapter 4 on environmental reporting and environmental reports. These three chapters correspond to the classification proposed by Neely who states that environmental performance measurement can be analysed at three levels: the level of individual physical EPIs, the level of the overall performance measurement system and the level of the relationship of this system with the external environment (Neely, 1993). Accordingly, Chapter 2 analyses the first level of physical environmental performance indicators, Chapter 3 focuses on the second level, the overall performance measurement system and Chapter 4 discusses the third of the above levels. Each of these chapters aims to evaluate the contributions made so far in this field of research, to define areas of theoretical and empirical weakness, and to identify trends in research activity in summarising the most relevant conclusions.

Chapters 5 to 7 describe the focal theory (Chapter 5), the methodology for variable definition, data collection and the resulting data set (Chapter 6) and the general strategy for the statistical analyses performed on the data set (Chapter 7). Starting from the literature review in Chapters 2 to 4, Chapter 5 develops and operationalizes the main hypotheses and research questions of this study. Chapter 6 then defines the variables used in the empirical study of environmental reports, environmental performance and the used physical indicators, based on the hypotheses developed in Chapter 5. In the case for the variables, which describe actual (physical) environmental performance, this is done separately for both sectors. Also, Chapter 6 describes the process of collecting data from the environmental reports of firms in the two sectors and countries and gives a first characterisation of the resulting data set. Chapter 7 then briefly describes the statistical analyses applied to the data set in subsequent chapters. The choice of analyses was based on the developed research hypotheses and the variables used in the study and will also be explained in more detail in this chapter.

Chapters 8 to 12 then go on to report the results of the analysis with regard to the hypotheses developed. After an exploratory data analysis, and a factor analysis of emissions in Chapter 8, the first hypothesis developed in Chapter 5 regarding the quality of environmental reports and the actual environmental performance of a company is tested in Chapter 9. Subsequently, in Chapter 10, the second hypothesis developed in Chapter 5 regarding the level of indicator use and the level of environmental performance is tested. The results of these tests then made it necessary to analyse in more detail the differences between companies certified under EMAS and ISO regarding their environmental performance and the quality of environmental reports under both standards in Chapter 11. Chapter 12 reports the results of a series of regression analyses, based on the results of the analyses reported in the previous chapters. Finally, to conclude the first part of this book, Chapter 13 summarises the results, draws some final conclusions for the link between environmental performance and reporting quality based on the results. It also provides some recommendations for improving reporting quality.

The second part of the book analyses the relationship between environmental and economic performance. Chapter 14 introduces this second part and the theoretical foundations for a (possibly non-linear) relationship and briefly sketches out the basic research questions and hypotheses. The next Chapter 15 reports the methodological aspects of the research. Subsequently results of the econometric analysis are presented in Chapters 16 (for the paper industry) and 17 (for the electricity sector) and are discussed in detail. The final Chapter 18 draws conclusions and raises some policy issues and recommendations. Chapter 19 provides the Appendices, followed by references and literature.

2.   Physical Environmental Performance Indicators

2.1   Introduction

This chapter aims to give an overview of possible theoretical concepts and practical implementations of physical environmental performance indicators (EPIs). Clearly physical EPIs themselves are not sufficient for environmental performance measurement but have to be combined with environmental condition indicators (e.g. sustainability, receptor or proxy environmental condition indicators) and management performance indicators (synonym: economic indicators). These groups of indicators can be related to each other on the basis of the OECD pressure-state-response model where physical environmental performance indicators represent pressures, states are reflected by environmental condition indicators and management performance indicators measure responses (Ditz & Ranganathan, 1997). However due to the fact that physical EPIs provide the link between management performance and environmental conditions, they are of special importance. After briefly defining the core terminology for physical EPIs, a theoretical concept is presented to classify them formally and as regards content. This is followed by a review of current initiatives aimed at the practical implementation of physical EPIs. From this conclusions are drawn as to the state of development and implementation of physical environmental performance indicators.

2.2   Core Definitions and Theoretical Classification of Environmental Performance Indicators

An environmental performance indicator can be defined as quantitative or qualitative information that allows us to evaluate, from an environmental viewpoint, a company's effecttiveness and efficiency in resource use (Bartolomeo, 1995). A physical indicator is one that is measured in scientific (as opposed) to monetary units. A quantitative indicator is one that can be measured on a ratio scale. Physical environmental performance indicators are EPIs that do not include monetary metrics (i.e. measuring units).

A recent matrix approach by an independent research organisation, the Institute of Ecological Economics Research, Berlin in Germany (Loew & Kottmann, 1996) classifies environmental performance indicators according to:

- Environmental effect categories (energy, transport, emissions, waste, waste water, products, waste water, land use),
- System boundaries (process, product, site, business unit, company or corporation) and
- Levels of analysis or representation (cause level, level of material and energy flows, cost level or impact level).

Performance indicators at the cost level can be derived from data on the materials and energy flow level if such flows cause costs, but to record such flow-induced costs and allocate them correctly to the polluting processes or activities, environmental cost and performance accounting is necessary.

It has to be noted that a classification like the one of Loew and Kottmann according to environmental effect categories is not free of double-counting as would be a differentiation in impact categories found in life-cycle assessment (LCA) such as e.g. global warming or ozone depletion (Heijungs, 1992). Therefore, although a classification into effect categories makes it possible to take into account resource inputs, it nevertheless causes difficulties for deriving sustainability or impact indicators. According to Loew and Kottmann (1996) different system boundaries for physical environmental performance indicators allow different perspec-

8

tives for analysis. In order to analyse a specific environmental effect category; for example, all site-, process and product-related EPIs can be applied. In order to identify improvements for processes and products, the EPIs for all environmental effect categories for one specific product or process can be combined in an analysis. Next to effect categories and system boundaries, the level of analysis is another classification criterion for environmental performance indicators. Here, on the causal level the sources of energy and material flows are represented. The level of materials and energy flows incorporates flow quantities that can be derived from site- or company-level, process-level and product-level mass and energy balances (which represent different forms of eco-balancing). These levels of analysis are captured by physical environmental performance indicators, which use genuinely physical metrics. Cost level indicators are indicators using monetary units. They therefore do not belong to the category of physical indicators anymore (Loew & Kottmann, 1996).

Finally, on the impact level, impacts of material and energy flows on e.g. climate, biosphere or atmosphere shall be represented in an aggregated way. This implies essentially an aggregation in overlap-free categories. Next to this a valuation of the actual impact of an emission on the environment has to be made. Examples for indicators on the impact level are the Critical Volume Approach (Bundesamt für Umwelt, 1991), the CML Method (Heijungs, 1992), Equivalence Coefficients (Müller-Wenk, 1978) and the NPI Global Warming Indicator (Tennant *et al.*, 1997). An exhaustive overview on impact-level indicators was compiled by Schaltegger and Sturm (1992; 1994; 2000). Table 1 summarises the described classification of indicators and the link between different types of indicators (e.g. physical, impact and condition indicators).

Table 1   Classification of environmental performance indicators

Effect categories (general)	Effect categories (specific)	System boundaries	Levels of analysis	Indicators used for measurement
Input indicators	Energy, Water, Materials	Product, Process Site, Business unit, Company, Corporation	Causal level (sources of flows)	Physical indicators
			Level of material and energy flows	Physical indicators
			Cost level	Economic indicators
Output indicators	Products, Waste, Emissions, Waste water		Impact level	Sustainability / Impact indicators
			Condition level	Environmental condition indicators
Infrastructure indicators	Transport, land use			

Source: Adapted from Loew and Kottmann (1996)

In the following section, after introducing a formal classification of physical environmental performance indicators, the most important initiatives currently addressing the development and implementation of physical EPIs are reviewed.

2.3 Formal Classification of Physical Environmental Performance Indicators

James and Bennett (1996), BMU/UBA (1997) and Siegwart (1992) give definitions for the different types of EPIs that can be found in practice. An absolute indicator is one that reports the total base data for a defined time period. Relative indicators are those that relate an environmental measure such as emissions, wastes or energy and material consumption to a measure of business activity or success such as production output, sales, value added or shareholder value. Relative indicators should be seen as complements to absolute EPIs. Figure 1 visualises these categories.

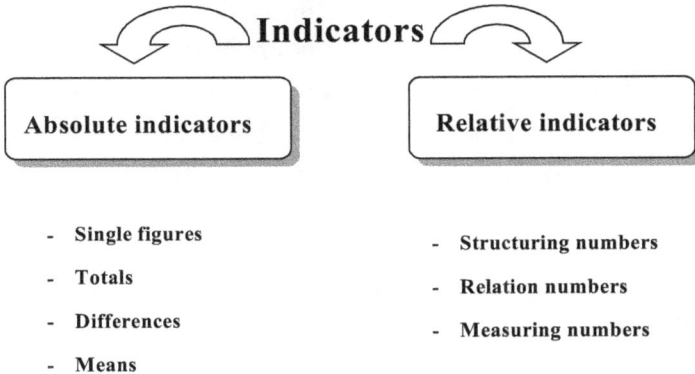

Indicators

Absolute indicators

- Single figures
- Totals
- Differences
- Means

Relative indicators

- Structuring numbers
- Relation numbers
- Measuring numbers

Source: modified from BMU/UBA (1995) and Siegwart (1992, p. 23)

Figure 1   Formal classification and types of environmental performance indicators

11

Absolute indicators serve as summary indicators of, for example, when derived from eco-balances and give an overview of total resource use, emissions and waste without being relative to production. At least in principle therefore data for these aggregated EPIs can be recorded during an eco-balance analysis. This analysis can also be more detailed to record further data that is relevant for the calculation of relative EPIs (e.g. the quantity of each type of energy used – fossil fuels, solar-thermal, photovoltaic, water, biomass, and wind energy).

Relative indicators are, for example, production- or service-specific ratios, energy and water quotas, material ratios and emission quotas. These relative indicators shall describe the most relevant environmental aspects of a firm's resource use, emissions and wastes, either relative to a unit of service (e.g. kg of product or per customer) or as a quota (i.e. energy/waste product as percentage of the total amount of energy or waste). Alternatively, Tyteca (1996) defines relative indicators as being the result of the comparison of a given variable/indicator with some pre-defined level e.g. worst or best practice, a standard derived from legislation, some quantity or quantities reflecting a firm's activity, or any specified target.

2.4 Review of Initiatives on Physical Environmental Performance Indicators

Generally initiatives on EPIs and more specific physical EPIs originate from sources as diverse as research institutes and universities, governments and governmental or super-national agencies, industry association, institutions and organisations in the financial sector, environmental organisations and other pressure groups, standardisation organisations and company-specific approaches. These and other organisations represent the interests of a variety of company stakeholders in various combinations.

This section discusses some recent initiatives and projects on physical environmental performance indicators. Several scholars in the field (Wehrmeyer & Tyteca, 1998; Wehrmeyer, 1998) and (Ranganathan, 1998) give an overview of current activities in the field. The review is based on a sample of initiatives that is summarised in Table 2.

Table 2:   Reviewed initiatives on physical environmental performance Indicators

Initiative	Source of Description
Association of Chartered Certified Accountants (ACCA) report	Bennett & James (1998)
Coalition of Environmentally Responsible Economies (CERES) Global Reporting Initiative	Coalition for Environmentally Responsible Economies (CERES) (1998)
EU Eco-Management and Audit Scheme (EMAS)	European Community (EC) (1993)
International Standards Organisation, Guideline ISO 14031	Technical Committee 207 (1996)
Eco-controlling and Eco-balancing	Azzone *et al.* (1996); Baumgartner & Rubik (1993); Young & Welford (1998)
German Federal Environment Ministry and German Federal Environmental Agency	Federal Environment Ministry & Federal Environmental Agency (1997)
World Business Council for Sustainable Development (WBCSD) "State of Play" Report on Eco-efficiency Metrics	Lehni (1998)

NATIONAL ROUND TABLE ON THE ENVIRONMENT AND THE ECONOMY (NRTEE)	National Roundtable on the Environment and the Economy (NRTEE) (1997)
EUROPEAN ENVIRONMENT AGENCY (EEA) WORKING PAPER ON ECO-EFFICIENCY INDICATORS	Gee & Moll (1998)
WORLD RESOURCES INSTITUTE (WRI) REPORT	Ditz & Ranganathan (1996)
STOREBRAND SCUDDER ENVIRON-MENTAL VALUE FUND (EVF)	Skillius & Wennberg (1998)
ICI Environmental Burden Index	ICI (1997); Wright *et al.* (1997)
DATA ENVELOPMENT ANALYSIS	Callens & Tyteca (1999)
The Business in the Environment Index of Corporate Environmental Engagement	Business in the Environment (BITE) (1996)

Each approach has its different strengths and weaknesses with regard to several criteria as e.g. performance measurement or performance management, applicability within an environmental management system or reliability of data collection.

The EMAS, ISO 14031 and German Environmental Agency initiatives are the most important ones in the field of performance management (which can be related to cost and performance accounting approaches and are directed to internal use within the company). EMAS is a Council Regulation allowing the voluntary participation by companies based in the industrial sector in a Community eco-management and audit scheme ((European Community, 1993). The ISO 14000 series is consisting of a series of standards and guidelines on environmental management systems. The ISO 14001 standard is specifying an environmental management system and gives guidance for its use. The standard is based on BS 7750 and the idea of continuously improving the environmental management system in order to achieve improvements in overall environmental performance of an organisation (Hunt & Johnson, 1992). The ISO 14031 draft standard provides guidelines on environmental performance evaluation (Technical Committee 207, 1996). ISO 14031 is well accepted amongst practitioners due to its proximity to the ISO 14001 and related standards on environmental management systems. The approach adopted in the German Environmental Agency's initiative is based on the EMAS and ISO standards and aims to make them more directly applicable to different industry sectors and especially SMEs by suggesting more specific indicators (Federal Environment Ministry & Federal Environmental Agency, 1997).

However its low level of standardisation and the variety of environmental performance indicators (EPIs) it proposes are seen as major weaknesses (Bennett & James, 1998). Similarly, EMAS helps to standardise the use of physical environmental performance indicators by defining reporting areas for environmental performance but unfortunately does not prescribe specific EPIs to characterise performance in these areas (Grafe-Buckens, 1997). An approach by the German Environmental Agency (Federal Environment Ministry & Federal Environmental Agency, 1997) goes further in this by suggesting core sets of environmental performance indicators for several types of companies and sectors using Eco-balancing as a means for arranging data. However this approach is more driven to performance management and therefore not applicable easily across sectors. A recent review (WBCSD, 2000) analysed the use of environmental performance indicators in firms based on environmental management systems standards. It was found that data focus is on the output side, with only limited information disclosed for the input side. System boundaries for data collection are usually drawn around own operations. The use of relative indicators is limited and a large variety of metrics is used. Data is typically normalised to product volume or industry-specific output units.

In contrast to the initiatives geared towards performance management those directed to performance measurement have rather distinct characteristics. The Coalition for Environmentally Responsible Economies (CERES) initiative for example stresses the need for standardisation and for a focus on a core set of indicators which should be sector specific. However it does not make suggestions for these indicators.

Similarly the World Resources Institute suggests standardisation and focus but proposes core areas around which to cluster environmental performance measurement which are materials use, energy consumption, non-product output (including pre-treatment wastes) and pollutant releases (including waste). The European Environment Agency (EEA) has adopted very similar key areas around which company-level indicators should be developed. In addition to that EEA calls for defined accounting and reporting procedures and for a link from company-level to economy-level environmental performance indicators. This micro-macro link could possibly achieved within the Systems of National Accounts currently employed in different countries.

The project by the World Business Council for Sustainable Development (WBCSD) aims to address sustainability, in particular Eco-efficiency by developing a concise set of indicators. For this purpose a review of possible aggregated indicators was carried out. This approach has been carried a step further by NRTEE who developed three aggregated indicators to measure Eco-efficiency. These indicators are the Toxic Release Index, the Resource Productivity Index and the Product and Disposal Cost to Durability Ratio.

Finally a recent report by the Association of Chartered Certified Accountants (ACCA) comes to similar conclusions with regard to standardisation of indicators and focus on core areas of performance which should incorporate sustainability and Eco-efficiency problems. It carries operationalization a bit further by pointing to the need for a life-cycle approach probably using a cascading flow of environmental performance information along the product chain (Ditz & Ranganathan, 1997).

2.5   Conclusions

In this section several physical EPI initiatives have been reviewed and classified. Some of these initiatives (EMAS, ISO, German Environmental Agency) are more aimed towards internal performance management whereas others are focussed on external performance measurement (WBCSD, AIChE, NRTEE) and predominantly formulate general or more specific guidelines on how to develop suitable physical environmental performance indicators (e.g. WRI, EEA, CERES, ACCA). From the review it became clear that the current practice of using EPIs is characterized by a low degree of standardization and the use of many different performance indicators that only rarely attempt to measure overall Eco-efficiency and almost never addresses overall sustainability. In contrast, the initiatives concerned with external performance measurement and more homogeneous use of environmental performance indicators point to the need of much stronger standardization, the use of a core set of indicators and life-cycle thinking that addresses Eco-efficiency and sustainability measurement.

Although some of the initiatives already consider sustainability, one future concern for the development of physical EPIs has to be the evaluation of the final environmental impact of a company which requires to focus more on impact measures and in particular on sustainability indicators (James & Wehrmeyer, 1996). This likely requires having an overlap-free classification in e.g. environmental media (soil, water and air) or in life-cycle analysis (LCA) effect categories (global warming, acidification, ozone depletion etc.). It also needs accepted and standardised protocols and procedures to calculate impact-level EPIs (e.g. sustainability EPIs). Examples for indicators proposed so far on the effect level are equivalency coefficients (Müller-Wenk, 1978), ecological footprints (Wackernagel & Rees, 1996) and critical volumes (Bundesamt für Umwelt, 1991).

3. Environmental Performance Measurement (EPM): The Overall Performance Measurement System

3.1 Introduction

Environmental performance measurement (EPM) can be defined as the measurement of the interaction between business and the environment (Bennett & James, 1997). As stated in the introduction, issues and perspectives of EPM can be analysed at the level of individual environmental performance indicators, the level of the overall performance measurement system and at the level of the relationship of this system with the external environment (Neely, 1993). The first level has been analysed in the previous chapter on physical environmental performance indicators and the last level is examined in the next chapter on environmental reporting and corporate environmental reports. The focus of this chapter is on the second level, the overall performance measurement system.

3.2 Driving Forces for Environmental Performance Measurement (EPM)

Several stakeholder interests drive the development of environmental performance measurement (James & Wehrmeyer, 1996). These aim mainly to support internal environment-related decision making (Business in the Environment (BITE), 1992), regulatory data requirements (Freedman & Jaggi, 1988), pressure group demands for detailed information and data (Seidel, 1988) and requirements of financial institutions, mainly banks, insurers and funds (Lascelles, 1993). Customer interests in environmental performance (Wells *et al.*, 1992) and requirements of environmental management standards (Gilbert, 1994) are also important drivers. Another set of driving forces stems from the final objectives of environmental performance measurement (EPM). Issues in this respect are (James & Wehrmeyer, 1996) whether EPM should be business-linked or solely oriented towards environmental improvement (James & Bennett, 1996), and related to that, if it should be oriented towards sustainability or towards more short-term, incremental improvements. This in turn points to the question if EPM should take a life-cycle approach or a more practical management-oriented one. Next to these three questions, there is the question if EPM should be more internally or externally-focused and finally the question about the relationship of EPM and environmental accounting (Gijtenberg *et al.*, 1996). Clearly these five forces are inter-related and also depend on stakeholder interests.

3.3   The Overall Performance Measurement System

Environmental performance indicators (EPIs) rarely stand alone and unlinked with each other.[6] Therefore, the issue is:

a) how to combine the EPIs into an overall performance measurement system covering all significant environmental aspects of a company's operations, and

b) what indicators are needed in an overall performance measurement system to measure the achievement of pre-defined environmental goals.

An overall performance measurement system can, for example, be mainly defined by industry sector (due to different environmental impacts specific to each sector), resulting in a set or sub-set of sector specific EPIs. Other determinants could be the level of public concern, the strict-

---

[6]   For example, the EPI initiatives presented in the sections to follow mostly put indicators in the framework of an overall system.

ness of national environmental legislation and the size of the organisation (James & Wehrmeyer, 1996; Schreiner, 1991). Yet another set of determinants could result from the relative importance of stakeholders to the company (Schaltegger & Figge, 2000). Much of the discussion is about identifying a suitable 'balanced scorecard' of monetary and non-monetary (i.e. physical) indicators (Bennett & James, 1997).

According to Loew and Kottmann (1996), a theoretically derived overall measurement system should predominantly consist of EPIs at the polluter level and the materials and energy flow level.[7] EPIs at these levels are usually sufficient to identify existing optimisation potentials on the operational level and are also sufficiently disaggregated to be linked to individual actors. However, for strategic planning decisions, EPIs on the effect level seem to be more appropriate although a mix of EPIs on the effect level and of EPIs on the materials and energy flow level seems to be most appropriate. The latter is the case, since such a mix would keep a balance between strategic and actor orientation. Nevertheless, the choice of an appropriate system depends very much on the approach taken towards EPM.

Broadly, six fields of application can be identified for environmental performance measurement systems (James & Bennett, 1996):

1. Economic approaches/applications which exclusively use monetary measures, mainly based on cost-benefit analysis (CBA) (May & de Motta, 1996; Leipert, 1989; Pearce & Turner, 1990);

---

[7]   The model proposed by Loew and Kottmann (1996) is discussed in more detail in Section 2.2 above.

2. Environmental accounting approaches/applications which aim to integrate environmental issues with mainstream accounting principles (Schaltegger & Burritt, 2000; Wallace & Parker, 1996);

3. Productive efficiency approaches/applications which use efficiency and financial measures (Tyteca, 1996; 1997; 1999);

4. Quality-based approaches/applications which combine total quality management (TQM) and environmental management (Willig, 1994);

5. Environmental auditing approaches/applications which focus mainly on the management of a company's environmental aspects (Ledgerwood *et al.*, 1993); and,

6. Ecological approaches/applications which predominantly apply life-cycle analysis (SETAC, 1992; Bundesamt für Umwelt, 1991; Spiller, 1996; Clift & Wright, 1999).

Wehrmeyer and Tyteca (1998) add two other more recent approaches, namely the Indicators of Sustainable Development approach (Dalal-Clayton *et al.*, 1994; Callens & Tyteca, 1999; Young & Rikhardsson, 1996) and the Systems approach based on the 'Industrial Ecology' concept (Ayres, 1996; Wernick & Ausubel, 1995).

3.4 Development Stages of the Overall Performance Measurement System in Environmental Performance Measurement

With regard to the development stages of the overall performance measurement system in EPM, Bennett & James (1998) describe three generations of environment-related performance measurement. Each of these corresponds to specific overall performance measurement systems characterised by groups of key indicators.

- The first generation is characterised by key indicators describing the business process, indicators on regulated emissions and wastes, and indicators for costly resources and compliance.

- In addition to these, the second generation of EPM includes indicators which reflect energy and materials usage/efficiency, significant emissions and wastes (regardless whether regulated or not), as well as financial and implementation indicators.

- The third generation of EPM is characterised by relative/comparative indicators, inclusion of the concept of eco-efficiency, the use of stakeholder, environmental condition and product indicators and application of a balanced scorecard of these indicators.

The relationship between the generation model of James and Bennett and their classification of environmental performance approaches is that different environmental performance approaches are used with varying intensity in the different generations of EPM. The ecological approach, for example, is predominantly found in third generation EPM, whereas the environmental auditing approach is mainly used in second generation measurement. The economic and the environmental accounting approach have initially been utilised in industry to a lesser extent, likely due to the issues surrounding monetarisation of physical environmental information. However, increasingly environmental accounting methods are adopted in industry (see Schaltegger & Burritt, 2000).

3.5 Conclusions: Perspectives and Trends for Overall Performance Measurement Systems

Several recent initiatives stress the needs for more standardisation (Ditz & Ranganathan, 1997; Bennett & James, 1998; CERES, 1998), measurement of sustainability (Wehrmeyer & Tyteca, 1998) and Eco-efficiency (WBCSD, 1998), life-cycle thinking (Bennett & James, 1998) and a narrower but deeper analysis of core areas of environmental performance (Bennett & James, 1998). Some initiatives point to the need to use sector-specific EPIs within an overall performance measurement system to mirror sector-specific environmental impacts (CERES, 1998).

A trend that emerges from these proposals is that increasingly the definition of Eco-efficiency coined by the World Business Council for Sustainable Development (Schmidheiny & Zorraquin, 1996) (as part of a broader definition of sustainable development) is adopted as a basis for developing indicators for environmental performance measurement (AIChE, 1997; NRTEE, 1997). Another emerging trend is the proposal of key resource flows/areas around which to cluster measurement and indicators (Gee & Moll, 1998; Ditz & Ranganathan, 1997). Areas proposed are quantities and types of materials used, quantities and types of energy consumption or generation, non-product output (i.e. waste generated before recycling) and pollutant release to air, water and land.

There are obviously relationships between the major trends, issues and developments of overall performance measurement systems for environmental performance measurement. The objective of achieving comparable, transparent and complete EPIs implies the need of adopting a standard set of universally reported indicators. This would allow tracking environmental performance of countries and regions (Ditz & Ranganathan, 1997) and could form a basis for consistent standards of accountability for business environmental performance. Such standardisation is likely to result from combined efforts of governments, international standards and ratings organisations and inter-firm co-operation, possibly facilitated by industry associations.

Environmental performance measurement as a practical means for internally measuring and externally communicating environmental performance improvements needs to serve diverse audiences with different information needs. One model could be a 'generic' environmental performance measurement that concentrates on key information which is relevant to all major target audiences (Azzone *et al.*, 1997). In that case the trend for standardisation would be closely tied with the need to focus on a core set of broadly applicable metrics which in turn makes it necessary to focus on core areas of performance. In order to incorporate all possible environmental effects these have probably to be defined in broad terms.

Currently the major issue on a strategic level is how to incorporate sustainability into environmental performance measurement (Wehrmeyer & Tyteca, 1998). This likely requires a focus on impacts rather than environmental aspects (Wehrmeyer, 1998) and combination of facility and community level information in order to relate micro-level data to macro-level performance for entire sectors, regions or nations. Next to this 'vertical' integration of EPM, there seems to be a clear need for more 'horizontal' integration by means of a cascading flow of information along the production chain to identify hidden flows of materials associated with downstream or upstream (Ditz & Ranganathan, 1997).

4. Environmental Reporting and Environmental Reports

4.1 Introduction to Environmental Reporting

Environmental reporting relates to the relationship of a company's overall environmental performance measurement system with the external environment (Bennett & James, 1997). A printed environmental report is only one tool for communication of environmental performance to the public (WICE, 1994) and should therefore be distinguished from the more general term of environmental reporting which describes the total of instruments for a company to disclose environmental information (Brophy & Starkey, 1996). Such instruments or channels of communication include meetings, newsletters, press releases and advertisements amongst others (Hunt & Johnson, 1992). Companies should first identify target audiences and their information needs and from that formulate an environmental communication strategy and identify the environmental information it should disclose. Within this strategy, for example, the use and format of an environmental report has then to be defined (Skillius & Wennberg, 1998)

4.2 Corporate Environmental Reports (CERs)

Corporate environmental reports can be defined as publicly available, stand-alone reports issued by companies to disclose environmental information (Brophy & Starkey, 1996). Gijtenberg *et al.* (1996) report two dimensions along which to classify environmental reports namely impetus (i.e. if reports stem from government mandate or from voluntary action) and scale (i.e. if reports are published at the site level, the company level, or the sectoral level). Site-level and company-level environmental reports are the two main types of environmental reports used, mostly in the context of voluntary environmental reporting[8]. The most prominent mandatory reporting schemes are the Toxic Release Index in the US, the UK Chemicals Release Inventory, the Federal Law on Ambient Air Protection (Bundesimmissionsschutzgesetz, BImSchG) in Germany and the Dutch Emissierregistratie-Industrie (ER-I).

The most widespread voluntary reporting scheme is the EU Eco-Management and Audit Scheme (EMAS). This scheme is based on site-level reporting and thus requires only a site-level environmental statement for which however very detailed guidelines exist as to what it has to include. EMAS is a regulated voluntary reporting scheme. It requires periodic publication of an environmental statement that requires among others an assessment of all significant environmental issues of relevance to the company's activities. Also a summary of figures on pollutant emissions, waste generation, consumption of raw material, energy and water, noise emissions and other significant environmental aspects of relevance to the company's is required (Skillius & Wennberg, 1998). This means that the scheme classifies environmental performance data according to environmental protection areas (e.g. energy, transport, emissions, waste, packaging, production, stock-keeping and water management). Full environmental statements under EMAS conforming to these requirements have to be prepared after an initial review or upon completion of a full audit which is usually required every three years (Skillius & Wennberg, 1998). Simplified environmental statements have to be produced annually under EMAS.

---

[8] Site-level environmental reports are often termed environmental statements, whereas company level reports are often referred to as environmental reports.

4.3 Practitioner's Opinion of Corporate Environmental Reports: Some Empirical Evidence

The fact that environmental reports have a variety of users (e.g. business users, financial institutions, consumers, communities and government agencies) makes different requirements very likely (Bennett & James, 1998). Although corporate environmental reports (CERs) and site-level environmental statements are the most common forms of environmental reporting, empirical research reveals scepticism about the value of corporate environmental reports. A survey of James and Bennett amongst environmental managers finds that only 7 % of the respondents totally agree that CERs are creating benefits that more than justify the resources invested in their production. Only about 38 % generally agree positively while the majority of respondents remains neutral or disagrees. Greater support was found for the statement that site reports create benefits that justify the resources invested in their preparation. Here 15% of the respondents agreed totally with this statement while about 60 % positively agreed with (Bennett & James, 1997).

One explanation for these results can be that site-level reports are more suitable to inform stakeholders that are interested in localised environmental impacts of plant operation (Gijtenberg *et al.*, 1996). However shareholders and regulators are likely to be more concerned about corporate environmental performance and should therefore prefer company-level CERs. This last argument is contradicting to some extent the empirical figures above as one would expect higher valuation of CERs. It can probably be explained by the fact that environmental reports are reported to be used mainly internally (Bennett & James, 1997) and that in this case the level of aggregation in a company-level report is too high to support environment-related decision-making.

The fact that most environmental reports are prepared for internal purposes also explains the problems attached to ranking (or: rating) of such reports. Ranking of environmental reports aims to provide an objective external evaluation of the quality of an environmental report in categories that allow comparison with other reports. Several studies have analysed the use and quality of environmental reports both at the company level (synonym: corporate) and at the site level. This includes benchmarking of corporate and site-level environmental reports (UNEP & Sustainability, 1998; future e.V. & IÖW, 1998), surveying the use of environmental reports for environment-related performance measurement (Bennett & James, 1998) and analyses how user requirements are met by (especially site-level) environmental reports (Grafe-Buckens, 1998). As most corporate environmental reports are published voluntarily or under regulated voluntary reporting schemes, a need for guidelines and benchmarking emerges in order to facilitate (or rather permit) ranking of the quality of environmental reports. Currently, legislation to regulate environmental reporting and introduce mandatory elements for environmental reports is discussed in the Netherlands. As well stricter and more specific requirements for environmental statements under the EMAS scheme are debated as part of the forthcoming revision of the EMAS legislation (Grafe-Buckens, 1998; Grafe-Buckens, 1997).

4.4   Conclusions

Although empirical work (Bennett & James, 1997) suggests scepticism about environmental reports which is mainly related to actual patterns of usage of them, these reports are one of the most direct and visible forms of a company to report its environmental performance and to show the firm's commitment to environmental protection or even sustainable development. However, the use of environmental reports moves at the same time towards a bifurcation point as there is increasing demand for more standardisation from stakeholders and users in order to allow for benchmarking or ranking and comparisons over time, firms, countries and sectors.

The empirical findings reported above reflect this uncertainty whether stand-alone environmental reports are a transitional stage with mandatory disclosure as the endpoint or if they themselves are the endpoint of an transition that will see increased standardisation (Gijtenberg *et al.*, 1996). Both directions seem to be possible given that the Netherlands are introducing a mandatory reporting scheme for large facilities which requires them to submit pollutant reports while parallel the European Commission intends to tighten the EMAS regulation by the year 2000 (Grafe-Buckens, 1998). One possible compromise that seems to emerge is therefore the introduction of quasi-mandatory environmental reporting within environmental management systems e.g. the EC EMAS scheme or the guidelines and standards of the ISO 14000 series.

However with the advent of electronic communication and global computer networks spreading out, some of the pioneers in the field (for example Dow Europe) already think of new ways of reporting environmental information in which stand-alone reports are not dominant any more thus making future developments more difficult to predict. This could overcome the fundamental problem of printed reports that they have to cater for a whole range of stakeholders and therefore run the risk to be superficial for each of them. Environmental reports accessible via the Internet could allow dynamic queries to corporate environmental databases that could provide individual stakeholders with tailored information. This could for example combine the advantages of site-level reporting for stakeholders interested in localised environmental impacts of production or facility operation with the interests of financial stakeholders as for example banks or insurers. The latter are usually more interested in aggregate information on corporate environmental performance or in very specific economic or physical indicators.

Current electronic environmental reporting mainly represents slight adaptations of printed environmental reports. Research identified about 120 electronic environmental reports ranging from separate internet-based reports and subsections of corporate web-sites to intranet-based sites aimed towards raising awareness amongst employees. It is recommended that electronic environmental reporting (EER) should be combined with other forms of environmental communication in an integrated approach. One of the major advantages of EER is that it can be updated continuously (Charter, 1998).

5 Focal Theory, Development and Operationalization of Hypotheses

5.1 Development of the Main Research Questions and Null Hypotheses

The literature review in Chapters 2 to 4 introduced the three areas that are the focus of this study: physical, quantitative environmental performance indicators, the overall performance measurement system and environmental reporting. As environmental performance indicators are usually used within an overall performance management system, no distinction between the two is going to be made for the purpose of this study[9]. However, different paradigms behind overall performance measurement systems are likely to influence the actual environmental performance of a firm. A ranking of environmental reports is based on the quality of the reports themselves only and does not inform about the physical environmental performance of a company. However, voluntary or mandatory environmental reporting benefits the physical environmental performance of a company as it forces companies to measure their environmental aspects (or even impacts) and communicate these to their stakeholders (Skillius & Wennberg, 1998). On the other hand empirical research suggests disillusionment at the low number of external readers of environmental reports and the low reliability of much of the data within these reports (IRRC, 1995). As a result of this they might not

---

[9]   This means that the set of indicators used by the majority of the firms covered in this study is taken as the overall performance measurement system. Other approaches are not feasible as they would not allow to compare the actual environmental performance of firms. However the quality of a company's overall performance measurement system is measured by assessing their use of the indicators in the environmental report.

be seen as relevant by company executives and therefore no correlation between their quality and level of environmental performance might be observable.

The core research question this analysis attempts to answer is, whether environmental reporting, the use of physical and quantitative environmental performance indicators and a company's actual environmental performance are positively correlated. To some extent it also aims to clarify the direction of causation between these three. For example, in the case that better environmental reporting *causes* better environmental performance it can be used as a valuable environmental management tool. On the other hand if no correlation would be found this would question the use of environmental reports, with fundamental implications for their credibility and consistency. In order to answer this basic question, the analysis has to be more detailed in order to assess the influences of various other factors. First of all the basic research question can be subdivided into the following two derived research questions and corresponding null hypotheses:

(i)   To what extent do the quality of environmental reports and the factual environmental performance of a company (based on the reported EPIs) correlate? The null hypothesis here would be that higher quality of a corporate environmental report does not correlate significantly with better physical environmental performance.

(ii)   Does a higher number or proportion of reported physical EPIs correlate at a significant level with higher physical environmental performance? The null hypothesis would be that there is no significant correlation.

In order to test these two derived null hypotheses without systematic or statistical errors, one has however to take into account possible differ-

34

ences between industries and individual companies depending on the external pressures different industries face or the proportion of small-medium sized enterprises in an industry (Bennett & James, 1997). Differences in national regulation can also lead to different approaches to environmental reporting and environmental performance measurement and its reporting in environmental reports of companies or site-level environmental statements (James & Wehrmeyer, 1996). This becomes especially evident from the fact that environmental reports in the US are usually much less factual, quantitative and informative due to the higher legal risk under the regulatory conditions in the US.

To account for other possible factors that influence the correlation between the quality of environmental reports (especially the level of use of quantitative physical indicators) and the actual environmental performance of a company, the following questions and hypotheses have to be addressed as well. This also aims, as far as possible, to assess the relative influence of the different factors. Three questions and factors seem to be especially relevant:

1) Does the use of EPIs (e.g. the total number) and/or the quality of CERs differ between the industries in each country?

Indicators often occur in the framework of an overall performance measurement system. In the case of the electricity sector commonly indicators for carbon dioxide, nitrogen oxides, sulphur dioxide, carbon monoxide and dust are used. For the paper sector a common system consists of indicators for chemical oxygen demand (COD), biological oxygen demand (BOD), nitrogen and phosphor contents in effluent and adsorbable organic halogens (AOX). Legal requirements are an important factor that influences the use of indicators. For example a company might be required to report COD but not BOD and consequently only uses an indicator for COD. In this respect the number of indicators used indicates if a firm uses them proactively as an internal management tool to improve environmental performance or only to monitor compliance with existing regulation.

With respect to the quality of environmental reports, a recent ranking exercise for environmental reports in Germany found that out of the 150 biggest German companies, only 57 produced a company-level environmental report and only a further 23 produced site-level environmental statements (future e.V. & IÖW, 1998). Out of the 57 reports, six were published by companies in the energy sector, but none by a firm from the pulp and paper sector (which could partly reflect the different levels of concentration in the two sectors). However, one of the 23 environmental statements has been published by a pulp and paper company[10]. A recent benchmarking survey (UNEP & SustainAbility, 1997; Elkington *et al.*, 1998) ranked the pulp and paper sector the same as utilities sector which might indicate that both sectors are similarly exposed to external pressure or tight legislation. Probably rather unexpectedly, the same survey ranked the average quality of corporate environmental reports (CER) over all sectors analysed clearly higher for the UK than for Germany, with scores of 74 out of 194 and 66 out of 194, respectively.[11] This result is tested for both the sectors and the countries. The null hypothesis would be that the quality of environmental reports in both sectors does not differ significantly and that the quality of the reports would not be significantly higher for the UK.

---

[10] Five of the six reports by energy companies and the environmental statement by the pulp and paper firm are included in this empirical study.

[11] Scores for the benchmark survey were based on the UNEP/SustainAbility fifty reporting criteria and the revised five-stage model originally developed by SustainAbility (UNEP & SustainAbility, 1996).

2)   What effect does different legislation and industry regulation in the UK and in Germany has on the level of actual environmental performance?

The hypothesis would be that the stricter German legislation should lead to a higher physical environmental performance of companies, regardless of the industry they belong to. Generally, legislation on air emissions is stricter in Germany for both sectors, whereas water legislation tends to be stricter for the pulp and paper sector in the UK (Wehrmeyer, 1998b). This would as well make likely a higher quality of environmental reports, if this is based on a rating scale for the reports that emphasises the use of performance indicators. However, the mandatory disclosure of environmental data in the UK through the CRI and the deregulation in Britain during the period from 1989 to 1998 might have influenced the situation for the UK in a way that explains the better quality of environmental reports from UK companies reported above (UNEP & Sustainability, 1997).

3)   Are quantitative physical environmental performance indicators (EPIs) used more in Germany due to its 'Eco-balancing' tradition as opposed to a more management-oriented 'Eco-controlling' approach in the UK?

The expectation would be that there is a significant difference in the use of quantitative physical performance indicators due to the influence of different scientific regimes (that is, the use of Eco-balancing), i.e. the use of quantitative physical indicators in Germany should be significantly higher than in the UK. A problem perceived in this respect is that it might be very difficult to separate a higher use of EPIs in one country due to stricter legislation from more intensive use resulting from a different scientific tradition.

5.2 Operationalization of Hypotheses

In order to test the above hypotheses using the data recorded from the environmental reports collected, it is necessary to operationalize these hypotheses. The two derived questions if a higher level of use of environmental performance indicators or a higher quality of environmental reports correlates significantly with higher physical environmental performance shall be addressed in different ways. In order to do this, the core concepts (i.e. environmental performance, quality of environmental reports and use of performance indicators) have to be further operationalized in more detailed variables. For these variables then statistical tests and analyses have to be defined as operationalized descriptions of the above research questions and hypotheses. In order to do this, in the following Chapter 6 the variables for the empirical study of the environmental reports are developed and described in more detail.

6 Methodology of the First Part

6.1 Definition of Variables

Three groups of variables have been identified, based on the main hypotheses developed to further operationalize them. These are general variables, variables that describe a company's environmental performance and variables that describe the quality of environmental reporting.

GENERAL VARIABLES

General variables are used to account for exogenous influences on environmental performance or reporting, that are not related to a correlation between these latter two. The number of employees is used as a proxy variable for company size. The general variables are summarised in the following table (numbers in brackets refer to SPSS coding).

Table 3:   List of general variables for the analysis of environmental
           reports

Variables	Value type	Value range
Firm	Integer	1..n
Year of publication	Integer	1994-95-96-97
EMAS verification	Binary	Yes (1) / No (2)
Full or part audit	Binary	Full (1) / Part (2)
Industry sector	Binary	Pulp & Paper (2) / Electricity (1)
Country	Binary	UK (2) / Germany (1)
Site- or company-level report	Binary	Site (1) / Company (2)
No. of employees	Integer	1..n
ISO 9000 certified	Binary	Yes (1) / No (2)
ISO 14000 certified	Binary	Yes (1) / No (2)
BS 7750 certified	Binary	Yes (1) / No (2)
Annual production	Real	1.. r

VARIABLES DESCRIBING ACTUAL ENVIRONMENTAL PERFORMANCE

The second group of variables are those that describe the actual environmental performance of a firm. These variables are essentially physical
environmental performance indicators for which values are available in

the environmental reports that are the base data for the study. Table 4 outlines these variables used for the paper industry.

From the table it becomes evident that the variables used for the paper sector are essentially from two environmental effect categories which are water pollution and air pollution. BOD and COD were included as they represent fairly independent aspects of the environmental performance of a company (Wehrmeyer, 1993). As far as possible, the above variables were taken directly from the environmental reports received. Where this was not possible, values were calculated on the basis of the values supplied in the reports.

For example, in a number of instances, only total annual values were supplied. In that case, these values were normalised using annual production to derive values per unit of production. This was necessary to ensure that site-level and company-level environmental performance can be compared as well as environmental performance for production units of different size on each level.

Although the most straightforward way to do this is to normalise resource consumption and emissions with production figures for the whole company and the site as described above, this might be problematic. One reason is the possibility that at some plants production stages take place with a higher environmental impact, than in others.

In such a case the (averaged) environmental performance of a whole company (i.e. the corporate environmental performance) cannot strictly be compared with site environmental performance for a production stage with high environmental impact.

However to ensure the homogeneity of the sample in this respect was beyond the scope of this analysis and it was therefore assumed, that production is fairly homogeneous over the sample.

Table 4: Variables used for the description of environmental performance

Variable	Sector use	Measurement unit
Annual Production	Paper, Electricity	Tonnes, MWh
Annual COD	Paper	Tonnes
Annual BOD	Paper	Tonnes
Annual Nitrogen	Paper	Tonnes
Annual Phosphate	Paper	Tonnes
Annual AOX	Paper	Tonnes
Annual water consumption	Paper	1000 cubic metres
COD per unit of production	Paper	Kg per tonne paper produced
BOD per unit of production	Paper	Kg per tonne paper produced
Nitrogen per unit of production	Paper	Kg per tonne paper produced
Phosphate per unit of production	Paper	Kg per tonne paper produced
AOX per unit of production	Paper	Kg per tonne paper produced
Water per unit of production	Paper	Cubic metres per tonne produced
Annual CO_2	Paper, Electricity	Tonnes
Annual SO_2	Paper, Electricity	Tonnes
Annual NO_x	Paper, Electricity	Tonnes
CO_2 per unit of production	Paper, Electricity	Kg per tonne paper produced

| SO$_2$ per unit of production | Paper, Electricity | Kg per tonne paper produced |
| NO$_x$ per unit of production | Paper, Electricity | Kg per tonne paper produced |

The pulp and paper industry transforms cellulose fibre paper raw material into a web of interconnected cellulose fibres, the final paper product using a variety of process options along the route from wood and paper (Smith, 1998). Although water requirements in the paper industry differ with products and processes (Gobbo, 1981) water is still the largest tonnage process material processed (Smith, 1998). Therefore water input is included as a variable to measure environmental performance.

For the purpose of this study, the pulp and paper industry is assumed to be homogenous enough in terms of products and processes to allow intra-industry comparisons (Wehrmeyer, 1993). This can be justified with the argument, that although a high level of product differentiation exists in the industry, this study is confined to two countries with very similar product requirements. A more detailed analysis however would have to account for process technology differences.

The same approach as for the paper sector was adopted for the electricity sector and led to the variables summarised in the following table.

Table 5:   Variables of environmental performance in the electricity
            industry

Variable	Sector use	Measurement unit
Annual production / total electricity generated	Paper, Electricity	Tonnes, MWh
Electricity generated from nuclear fuel sources	Electricity	Percentage share of total electricity generated
Electricity generated from wind	Electricity	Percentage share of total
Electricity generated from coal	Electricity	Percentage share of total
Electricity generated from gas	Electricity	Percentage share of total
Electricity generated from water	Electricity	Percentage share of total
Electricity generated from oil	Electricity	Percentage share of total
Electricity from other sources	Electricity	Percentage share of total
Annual CO_2	Paper, Elect.	Tonnes
Annual SO_2	Paper, Electricity	Tonnes
Annual NO_x	Paper, Elect.	Tonnes
CO_2 per unit of production	Paper, Electricity	Kg per tonne paper produced
SO_2 per unit of production	Paper, Electricity	Kg per tonne paper produced
NO_x per unit of production	Paper, Electricity	Kg per tonne paper produced

Measurement of environmental performance in the electricity sector is based on air pollution and resource use measures. Again, as far as possible per-unit-of-production emissions were taken directly from the environmental reports. Where this was not possible, total annual emission data was normalised using total annual production. Similarly, as far as possible, generation shares were taken directly from the reports. Where this was not possible they were either calculated from data available in the reports or the fuel shares were used as a first approximation. With the variables introduced above, the concept 'environmental performance' can be operationally defined as the performance measured by this set of environmental performance indicators (EPIs) which have been consistently chosen from accepted initiatives or projects to develop EPIs or EPI systems. In a similar way, a set of variables can be identified for assessing the quality of company's environmental reports.

VARIABLES FOR THE QUALITY OF ENVIRONMENTAL REPORTING

This group of variables is probably the most problematic one as a variety of suggestions to assess environmental reporting and in particular environmental reports exist, but despite of this no generally accepted standard exists (Skillius & Wennberg, 1998). Furthermore most of the current assessment schemes have the rationale to benchmark environmental reports, but not to relate the use of physical environmental performance indicators in an environmental report (and the quality of environmental reporting in general) with actual environmental performance of a company. Therefore, for the purpose of this study it is suggested to use a set of variables that is adapted to the scope as well as to the sectors examined in the survey. These variables are consistent with the criteria of other accepted benchmarking schemes (KPMG, 1996; UNEP & Sustainability, 1996, UNEP & Sustainability, 1997; WICE, 1994; BITE,

1996; CERES, 1998). The following table outlines the variables chosen which are explained in more detail afterwards.

Table 6: Variables describing the quality of environmental reporting

Variable	Sector use	Measurement unit / metric
Length of environmental report	Paper, Electricity	No. of pages
Water performance indicators	Paper	No. of indicators used: BOD, COD, TSS, AOX, pH, N, P
Air performance indicators	Paper, Electricity	No. of indicators used: CO_2, NO_x, SO_2, CO, Dust
Length of environmental policy	Paper, Electricity	No. of single-column lines
Discussion of sustainability	Paper, elect.	Binary (Yes / No)
Reporting on CO_2 emissions	Paper, elect.	Binary (Yes / No)
Reporting on NO_x emissions	Paper, Electricity	Binary (Yes / No)
Use of Eco-balancing	Paper, Electricity	Binary (Yes / No)
Use of time-series	Paper, Electricity	No. of years reported backwards

The length of the environmental report is used as a proxy quality indicator for the quality of environmental reporting. The length of the environmental policy was counted as zero lines if the environmental policy was not included.

The number of indicators used in a report was chosen to be bigger than the number of emissions recorded, but kept small enough to be compared over the whole sample. Sustainability reporting, that is, a discussion of the issues surrounding sustainable development and the consequences that can be drawn from this for the company was measured by four qualitative (i.e. binary) indicators.

The first one is if discussion of sustainability took place in the environmental report. By this it is understood that a separate chapter or another form of specific reporting on sustainability (for example 'sustainability headlines' on each page as in the report of one of the electricity companies) was included in the report.

A second measure chosen to assess sustainability reporting was, if the total annual CO_2 emissions from the company's or sites activities were reported. CO_2 is a major contributor to global climate change, a long-term problem that is genuinely related to sustainable development and the corresponding major transformation of the industrial society (Tennant et al., 1997). CO_2 is also to a much lesser extent involved in other (non-overlapping) impact categories as e.g. stratospheric ozone depletion or acidification (Udo de Haes, 1996), so that it can be seen as being mainly a proxy measure for addressing global sustainability.

The third measure used to assess sustainability was if NO_x emissions were reported or not. NO_x refers to rather local forms of environmental pollution, which however have long-term effects. It can therefore be taken as a proxy measure for a company addressing local sustainability. For this reason it is crucial to address these aspects when aiming for sustainable development. Finally the use of Eco-balancing as a tool for data collection and presentation was used as a variable to measure the extent of sustainability reporting as it is a very structured and sophisticated form of material and energy flow balancing that comes very close to environmental accounting concepts[12]. These four binary variables where then given equal weight and aggregated into a single number by adding up the scores for each single measure (the individual measure scores were either zero or one depending on if the criterion for the category was fulfilled or not).

The result of this aggregation exercise is a 'sustainability reporting score' with companies being able to score between zero and four on this 'sustainability reporting scale'.

Admittedly the variables used have a bias towards environmental sustainability as the categories of economic and social sustainability are addressed only implicitly. However this seems to be justified as at least implicitly aspects of these two categories are addressed. Additionally, there is interdependence between all three categories e.g. in the sense that a polluted environment likely impacts negative on social sustainability (as e.g. habitants move out of the polluted neighbourhood and consequently social structures deteriorate).

Using the variables outlined and defined in Table 6, the concept 'quality of a CER' can be operationally defined by evaluating the CER based on them. Again it has to be emphasised that these variables are based on

---

[12] Inclusion of a mass-balance or Eco-balance sheet in the environmental report is used as a criterion in the UK ACCA award scheme (ACCA, 1998). Next to it being a very stringent data collection tool, it is assumed to be indicative for supplying concise and complete primary data on environmental effects which allows verification of environmental performance by the reader of the environmental report.

accepted benchmarking guidelines or on consistently used parts of such guidelines.

6.2   Data Collection and Characterisation of the Data Set

To analyse the relationship between actual environmental performance, the use of physical environmental performance indicators (EPI) and corporate environmental reporting, data from the collected company-level and site-level environmental reports and annual statements published in the pulp and paper and electricity industries in Germany and the UK was used. The two sectors have been chosen, as a high number of sites are registered under EMAS and therefore produce validated environmental statements. From the environmental reports data on the variables outlined in the previous section has been collected which form the base data set for the following analysis. Data was collected from company-level, stand-alone environmental reports and from site-level environmental statements published under the EMAS scheme for both sectors and both countries. The reports in Germany predominantly have been published under the EMAS scheme, whereas this was only very rarely the case for Britain. The following table summarises information on data collection, response rates and usability of the reports.

Table 7: Characterisation of the data set

Sector and Country	Reports reques-ted	Reports received		Reports used for data collection		Reports with full set of data	
		EMAS	Non-EMAS	EMAS	Non-EMAS	EMAS	Non-EMAS
Paper, UK	8	2	6	2	6	0	2
	14.3%	6.7%	66.7%	8%	66.7%	0%	50%
Paper, Germany	48	30	3	23	3	5	2
	85.7%	93.3%	33.3%	92%	33.3%	100%	50%
Paper total	*56*	*32*	*9*	*25*	*9*	*5*	*4*
	100 %	*100%*	*100%*	*100%*	*100%*	*100%*	*100%*
Paper to-tal aggre-gate	*56*	*41*		*34*		*9*	
	100 %	*73.2% of 56*		*60.7% of 56*		*16.1% of 56*	
Electricity, UK	9	0	18	0	16	0	16
	25.7%	0%	69.2%	0%	84.2%	0%	84.2%
Electricity, Germany	26	9	8	8	3	6	3
	74.3%	100%	30.8%	100%	15.8%	100%	15.8%
Electricity total	*35*	*9*	*26*	*8*	*19*	*6*	*19*
	100%	*100%*	*100%*	*100%*	*100%*	*100%*	*100%*
Electricity total aggre-gated	*35*	*35*		*27*		*25*	
	100%	*100% of 35*		*77.1% of 35*		*71.4% of 35*	

The table shows that a higher total number of reports have been received from the paper sector. However, the quality of reports was better in the electricity sector. Whereas in the paper sector the majority of reports are environmental statements prepared under EMAS, the majority of reports in the electricity sector were not published under the EMAS scheme. Generally the response rate was very high. The 100% response rate in the electricity sector results to a small extent from the fact that some firms sent reports for different years, whereas a small number of firms in that sector did not respond at all.

7.   Approach to the Statistical Analysis

The approach to the statistical analysis was to first perform an exploratory data analysis of the data set with respect to the most relevant variables in Chapter 8. Prior to this a final data check (sum checks for all
variables to ensure accurate data transfer and spot checks for outliners
and extreme values) was carried out.

In order to compare mean values for any two of the variables recorded
for the firms in the sample, the t-test is used during the exploratory data
analysis in Chapter 8.1. This is a statistical test for comparing the average
levels of two samples of interval tests the difference between two means
for significance (Kinnear & Gray, 1997). For this study all factors are
between-subjects, i.e. each firm is tested only once and therefore factors
can only vary from one subject to the other, not within one subject. This
means that the environmental performance (e.g. a typical emission figure) can only vary from one firm to another, but not within one firm.
Therefore the independent samples t-test was used. However to apply
the test to the data of the study it has to be ensured that it meets the assumptions of the test. These are that the data have been derived from
normal distributions with equal variance. If exploratory data analysis
reveals that the assumptions for a t-test are seriously violated, than a
non-parametric test has to be chosen instead which does not have specific assumptions about population distributions and variance (Kinnear
& Gray, 1997).

For more detailed testing, instead of applying t-tests the use of one-way
analysis-of-variance (ANOVA) to estimate correlations and their significance is strongly advocated to avoid artificially increased correlations.
ANOVA's were accordingly carried out in Chapter 8.2 to confirm the

results from exploratory data analysis and t-tests regarding air and water emissions for both sectors and countries.

After the exploratory data analysis, factor analyses were carried out to identify principal components for air and water emissions in Chapter 8.3. This was subsequently used as input for testing the first hypothesis regarding the quality of environmental reports and the actual environmental performance of a company in Chapter 9. This first hypothesis developed in Chapter 5.1 was then tested in Chapter 9.1, and subsequently, in Chapter 9.2 an ANOVA for the quality of environmental reports was carried out to confirm the results.

The second hypothesis developed in Chapter 5.1 regarding the level of indicator use and the level of environmental performance was tested in Chapter 10. After an introduction in Chapter 10.1, the hypothesis was tested for air emissions and air emission indicators in Chapter 10.2 for both sectors together as well as separately for each of the electricity and paper sectors. In Chapter 10.3 the hypothesis was then tested for water emissions and water emission indicators for the pulp and paper sector.

The results of Chapter 10 then made it necessary to analyse in more detail the differences between companies certified under EMAS and ISO regarding their environmental performance and the quality of environmental reports under both standards. This was carried out in Chapter 11.

In Chapter 12, finally, a series of regression analyses is carried out, in order to assess the relative importance of different variables from the data set on the level of emissions and hence the environmental performance of the firms in the sample. This also includes analyses aimed at determining the best predictors for air and water emission levels.

8. Exploratory and Preparatory Data Analysis

8.1 Exploratory Data Analysis and t-Tests

In order to ensure the applicability of further statistical analyses, an exploratory data analysis was first applied to the data set. As a first step boxplots for air emissions were examined to verify that the ranges for the paper and electricity industry are comparable.

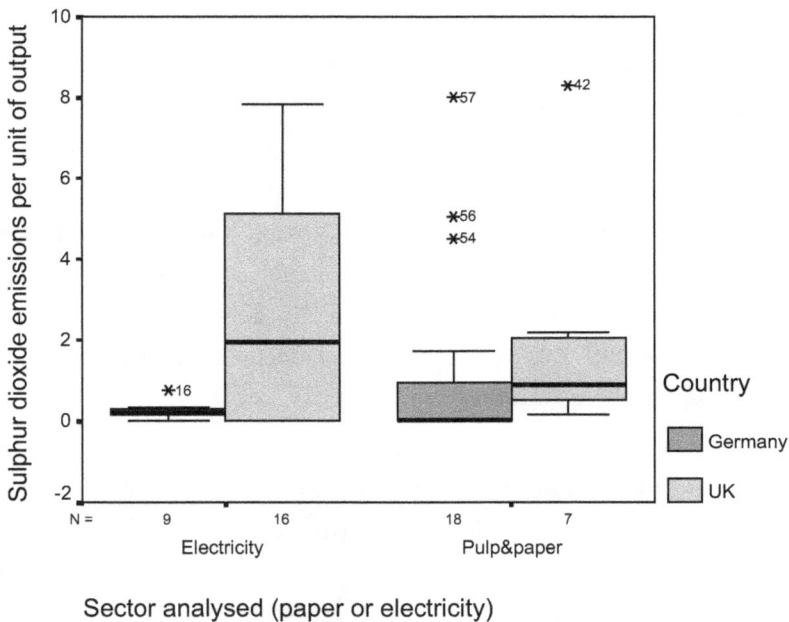

Figure 2: Boxplots for sulphur dioxide emissions per unit of output by sector clustered by country

Prior to the analysis, all environmental performance variables (measured as total emissions) were standardised with annual production output to arrive at efficiency measures. The Figures 2 to 4 each show boxplots for the three air emission efficiencies analysed. The black bar in each box denotes the median value, whereas the boxes denote the inner two quartiles around the median, i.e. the inter-quartile range containing 50% of the values. The whiskers denote the outer two quartiles around the median, i.e. they extend from the box to the highest and lowest values, respectively, whilst excluding outlier and extreme values. The boxplots therefore also show the distribution of the variable in question and thus also to some degree how well the variable conforms to a normal distribution. Outlier values are identified by a circle and extreme values by an asterisk and the number of the observation the value belongs to in the data set. Significant differences between two boxplots can commonly be identified by missing (or almost missing) overlap of the whiskers of these two boxplots. An analysis of the frequency distributions of the variables for carbon dioxide, sulphur dioxide and nitrogenous oxide emissions per unit of output for the firms analysed suggests that the assumption that these emissions are normally distributed is likely to be partly violated. Still it is assumed that the violations are small enough to apply t-tests to these variables.

For the SO_2 emissions per unit of output the application of an independent samples t-test found that the mean values of this variable are significantly lower for the electricity in Germany compared to the United Kingdom. No other significant differences between the emission levels were found for sulphur dioxide. Thus, for SO_2 emission efficiency, only country-related significant differences for one of the two sectors analysed could be identified. The next diagram shows the same boxplot for carbon dioxide emissions.

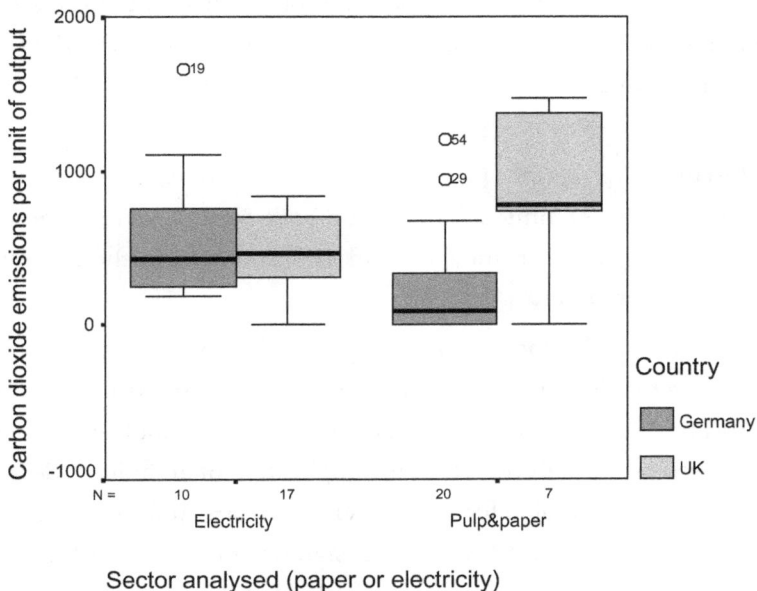

Figure 3:   Boxplots for CO₂ emissions per unit of output by sector
             clustered by country

An independent samples t-test showed that the mean CO_2 emissions per unit of output for the electricity sector in the United Kingdom are significantly lower (at the 0.01 level) than in the pulp and paper sector (equal variances assumed). As well, the mean CO_2 emissions per unit of output were significantly different (at the 0.05 level) for the pulp and paper sector in the UK and in Germany (equal variances not assumed), with the latter having the lower mean. These results confirm the conclusions that are suggested by the above diagram.

In the case that a parametric test (as e.g. the t-test) is not applicable, a nonparametric test might be considered. In the case of the independent samples t-test, the Mann-Whitney test is the nonparametric equivalent

(Kinnear & Gray, 1997). The application of this test to the same tested, grouping and clustering variables as for the parametric test yielded the same qualitative results i.e. significance at the 0.01 and 0.05 levels, respectively.

Next to the sector-specific CO_2 emissions per unit of output, also the total CO_2 emissions per unit of output for both sectors were significantly lower in Germany than they were in Germany. No further, significant differences were found.

Finally, the boxplot for the nitrogenous oxide emissions was analysed. Again, a set of independent samples t-tests was carried out to identify significant differences within sectors and between countries. As for the SO_2 emissions per unit of output the application of an independent samples t-test to the variable for the NO_x emissions per unit of output found that the mean value of this variable is significantly lower for the electricity sector in Germany compared to the United Kingdom. However, this has to be put in context by also analysing the fuel mix for both countries. In the case that coal would be a significantly higher fuel input in the United Kingdom, compared to Germany this would be a likely explanation for higher NO_x emissions in Britain. Consequently, this difference would be less much due to differences in the relevant legislation or the differences in quality of environmental management in both countries. However it was found (using again t-tests) that neither fossil fuel input (coal, gas and oil) has a significantly higher share of the total electricity generation in both countries. This makes legal differences a more likely explanation.

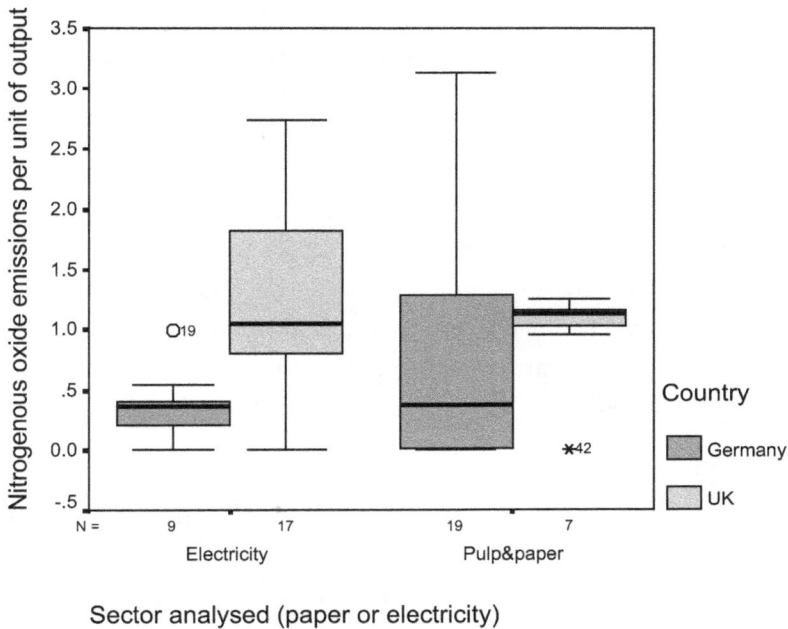

Figure 4: Boxplots of NO_x emissions per unit of output by sector clustered by country

Next to significant differences in the electricity, also the NO_x emissions per unit of output are significantly different (at the 0.05 level) for both countries and are significantly lower in Germany. Given the previous analysis, it is more likely now, that this is due to differences in the regulatory regime and strictness of environmental legislation. Especially the fact that all three air emissions for both sectors are significantly lower in Germany than in the United Kingdom strongly points to the influences of differences the strictness of environmental legislation.

Given this and that no significant difference in the mean values of emission efficiencies were found (except for CO_2) between the two sectors, it was concluded that differences in emission efficiencies are determined by country rather than by sector membership. This makes legal differences a more probable explanation of the results in that stronger environmental legislation in Germany may be a determining factor for better corporate environmental performance in Germany.[13] Especially the fact that more than one air emission is significantly lower in Germany than in the UK supports such an often argued influence of environmental legislation. Based on these considerations it seems likely that differences in the stringency of environmental regulation concerning air emissions are an important explanatory factor for the significant differences found in environmental performance with regard to air emission efficiencies between the two countries.

8.2   ANOVA for Emissions

In the case that a t-test expresses significance, one can reject the null hypothesis i.e. that there is difference between the two population means. However, the t-test cannot be used to evaluate a hypothesis about three or more population means (Kinnear & Gray, 1997). In such a case, applying a series of t-tests (i.e. multiple comparisons) leads to the problem that the probability of at least one test showing significance even when the null hypothesis is true (i.e. that there is no difference between the different population means) is higher than the conventional significance level (Gravetter & Wallnau, 1996). In this situation, a one-way analysis of variance (ANOVA) can be applied to the data. If the ANOVA test gives significance, than one can conclude that there is a difference somewhere among the means, however it cannot be said that any particular comparison is significant. One-way ANOVA tests were carried out over both sectors and countries to confirm the above results regarding countries

---

[13]   See Handler (1997) and Scherer (1997) for basic descriptions of the respective regulatory regimes with regard to environmental legislation in general and air emissions regulation in particular.

and sectors. The One-way ANOVA which was carried out for the variables for CO_2, SO_2 and NO_x emissions with the country variable as a factor revealed that all three emission variables were significantly correlated with the country at the 0.01 level (2-tailed). The mean values for these three variables were all significantly higher in the United Kingdom than in Germany as summarised in the following table.

Table 8:   One-way ANOVA for the air emission variables and countries

Country were company is located	Mean CO_2 emissions per unit	Mean SO_2 emissions per unit	Mean NO_x emissions per unit
Germany	353.28 t per unit	0.87 t per unit	0.61 t per unit
United Kingdom	583.61 t per unit	2.47 t per unit	1.13 t per unit
Total	455.65 t per unit	1.61 t per unit	0.85 t per unit
Significance of mean differences	Sig. = 0.049 F = 4.048	Sig. = 0.017 F = 6.077	Sig. = 0.015 F = 6.325

Another ANOVA test was carried out for the three air emission variables with the sector as a factor. In this case, no significant correlation could be identified.

Table 9:   One-way ANOVA for the air emission variables and sectors
analysed

Sector company is operating in	Mean CO_2 emissions per unit	Mean SO_2 emissions per unit	Mean NO_x emissions per unit
Electricity	495.96 t per unit	1.78 t per unit	0.90 t per unit
Pulp and paper	415.34 t per unit	1.43 t per unit	0.79 t per unit
Total	455.65 t per unit	1.61 t per unit	0.85 t per unit
Significance of mean differences	Sig. = 0.469 F = 0.470	Sig. = 0.610 F = 0.264	Sig. = 0.603 F = 0.274

From this it can be concluded, that the significant difference for emission levels is determined by the country rather than the sector. This partly supports the hypothesis that the strong environmental legislation in Germany is a very important factor determining corporate environmental performance.

8.3   Factor Analysis for Air and Water Emissions

In order to identify underlying trends, which may explain the pattern of correlation within the set of observed variables, several factor analyses were carried out. Factor analysis aims for data reduction, by identifying a small number of factors which explain most of the variance observed in the total number of variables (Newbold, 1991). A factor analysis was carried out for the three air emission variables, i.e. carbon dioxide (CO_2), sulphur dioxide (SO_2) and nitrogenous dioxide (NO_x). The principal factor method was used to extract the factors. These factors were then rotated using the Varimax method to achieve a 'simple structure' correlation.

The following table shows the communalities for the whole data set and for both sectors separately (the values for the component matrix are reported in brackets).

Table 10: Communalities for factor analysis of sectors for air emission variables

Variable	Both sectors	Electricity sector	Paper sector
CO_2 emissions	0.362 (0.602)	0.515 (0.718)	0.290 (0.538)
SO_2 emissions	0.795 (0.892)	0.817 (0.904)	0.747 (0.864)
NO_x emissions	0.803 (0.896)	0.933 (0.966)	0.665 (0.815)

Similarly, a factor analysis for the three air emission variables was carried out for the two countries separately. The results for this are summarised in the following table.

Table 11: Communalities for factor analysis of countries for air emission variables

Variable	Both countries	Germany	United Kingdom
CO_2 emissions	0.362 (0.602)	0.050 (0.224)	0.465 (0.682)
SO_2 emissions	0.795 (0.892)	0.908 (0.953)	0.761 (0.872)
NO_x emissions	0.803 (0.896)	0.955 (0.977)	0.705 (0.840)

The factor analyses carried out for the three air emissions variables (CO_2, SO_2 and NO_x) showed that for both sectors that the SO_2 and NO_x emissions were those factors that explained most of the variance observed. This was more so for the paper sector in both countries than for the electricity sector. The differences observed were small enough to generalise over both sectors. As the data set proved to be homogenous enough to generalise over both sectors and countries, in a final step, the factor scores of each company for the three air emission variables were calculated to be used in further statistical analysis.

In the same way, a factor analysis was carried out for five water emission variables in the pulp and paper sector. These variables were biological oxygen demand (BOD), chemical oxygen demand (COD), and phosphorous (P) and nitrogen (N) emissions into water and adsorbable organic halogens (AOX). From the results it can be assumed that the variables do not suffer from multi-collinearlity or singularity. As well the KMO measure of sampling adequacy was high enough to proceed safely with the analysis and Bartlett's test of sphericity confirmed that the matrix is most likely not to be an identity matrix. Based on these results it was proceeded with the factor analysis to extracting the communalities using the principal factor method. These were then rotated using again the Varimax method. In a final step, the factor scores for each company were calculated.

9. Testing of the First Main Hypothesis

9.1 Correlation between Environmental Report Quality and Environmental Performance

In the following section, the two derived hypotheses developed in Chapter 5.1 shall be tested. The first hypothesis to be tested is that a higher quality of environmental reports correlates significantly with better physical environmental performance. In order to test this hypothesis, the normalised air and water emissions (i.e. the air and water emissions per unit of output) were analysed with regard to possible correlation to the variables describing the quality of the environmental reports in the sample. The variables used to describe report quality were the length of the report (in pages), the length of the environmental policy (in lines), the average time for which emissions were reported back in the report (in years) and score on the sustainability rating scale (out of four). Additionally to these interval or nominal (in the case of the rating scale and the time reported back) variables, point-biserial correlations (Rpb) were also calculated for several air and water emission variables and two nominal variables. These two nominal variables were if an Eco-balance used in the environmental report and if sustainability was discussed in a separate section of the report. The emission variables used were the air and water factor scores calculated in the above factor analysis, the air emission variables for carbon dioxide, sulphur dioxide and nitrogenous dioxide (each separately) and the water emission variables for biological oxygen demand (BOD), chemical oxygen demand (COD), phosphorous (P) and nitrogen (N) emissions, adsorbable organic halogens (AOX) and water input into production. Correlation coefficients (for the Pearson correlation R) for air emissions and report quality were calculated for both sectors together, whereas correlation for water emissions and report quality could only be calculated for the pulp and paper sector. The results are summarised in the following table.

Table 12: Correlations for air emissions and report quality

Report quality variable / Emission variable	Use of an Eco-balance in the environmental report	Average time for which emissions were reported back
Air emissions factor score	Rpb = -0.355 Significant at 0.05 level (2-tailed)	R = 0.330 Significant at 0.05 level (2-tailed)
Sulphur dioxide emissions per unit of output separately	Rpb = -0.310 Significant at 0.05 level (2-tailed)	R = 0.284 Significant at 0.05 level (2-tailed)
Nitrogenous oxide emissions per unit of output separately	Rpb = -0.303 Significant at 0.05 level (2-tailed)	No significant correlation
Nitrogen emissions into water per unit of output	Rpb = -0.504 Significant at 0.05 level (2-tailed)	No significant correlation

No significant correlation could be found between any of the interval scale variables. The only significant correlation for the factor scores were found for the binary variable of whether an Eco-balance was used in the report and the nominal variable recording the average time for which emissions were reported back in the report, measured in years. However, only in the case of the use of an Eco-balance was this correlation negative, indicating that its use possibly reduces air emissions. In the case of the average time emissions were reported backwards, the correlation was positive, indicating that this element of an environmental report does not influence positively the environmental performance of a firm. This is of particular interest, as usually time-series reported show a falling emission trend, sometimes for the last five to seven years. The fact that no significant negative correlation could be established might point to conclusion, that these reductions are rather not due to proactive environmental management in these industries, but rather to exogenous factors as for example the tightening of legislation, emergence of a recession or investment in, and installation, of modern production technologies to increase competitiveness.

If the results for the sector scores are disaggregated to the individual air emissions it becomes clear that carbon dioxide emissions are not at all significantly correlated to the quality of environmental reports. The strongest correlation found is that for sulphur dioxide emissions, which is significant for both, the use of an Eco-balance as well as the average time emissions were reported backwards. In the case of the latter this is also the only significant correlation for air emissions, which means that the correlation established for the air factor score is essentially the correlation between sulphur dioxide emissions and the average time emissions were reported backwards. This is consistent with the above argument concerning exogenous factors and their effect on the reduction of air emissions, as sulphur dioxide is subject of considerable legislation and, to a large extent due to this, several forms abatement technology for sulphur dioxide emissions have been developed.

Concerning the use of an Eco-balance in the environmental report, analysing the correlation to the individual air emissions it can be found that a significant negative correlation only exists for nitrogenous oxide emissions and sulphur dioxide emissions. However this also means, that not a single emission is causing the correlation for the air factor score which points more strongly to the possibility, that the use of an Eco-balance in an environmental report is a possible indicator for above-average or even good environmental performance. As this is the only quality variable that expresses a negative correlation this would also be a very robust indicator. One could make the theoretical argument that Eco-balancing is probably the most sophisticated form of input-output analysis currently used in environmental management to establish the environmental effects of firms and that an Eco-balance would as well be a very sound basis for internal Eco-controlling (i.e. internal decision making aimed at improving environmental performance). This suggests for the Eco-balance to be useful for reporting the actual environmental performance of a firm as well as for assessing the quality of environmental performance from the environmental report. Also, it is further supported by the fact that the only significant correlation between water emissions and environmental quality measures for a report that could be established was a negative correlation between the use of an Eco-balance in the report and the nitrogen emissions into water per unit of output. Given that this established a significant negative correlation for both environmental media analysed (air and water) this seems to further support the result.

9.2   ANOVAs for Quality of Environmental Reports in Sectors and Countries

Similar to the above ANOVA analysis for emission differences in countries and sectors, ANOVAs were carried out to identify possibly significant reporting differences between the two countries and sectors. Subsequent to reporting their results, the core research question regarding the association between environmental report quality and corporate environmental performance is addressed. To measure the quality of environmental reports, the length of the report (in pages), the length of the environmental policy (in full page width-equivalent lines) and a 'sustainability reporting index' described at the end of Chapter 6.1 were used.[14] Variables for the use of quantitative environmental performance indicators were not used separately, since the 'sustainability reporting index' includes them to some extent. The length of an environmental report can be considered in a first approximation as a measure of the information content of the report and hence the level of detail of a firm's environmental reporting. The length of the environmental policy contained in the report is to considerable degree proportional to the level (i.e. the depth and breadth) of corporate commitment to environmental management in general and as part of this also to firms' environmental

---

[14]   The 'sustainability reporting index' consists of the components Eco-balance use, use of CO_2 and NO_x indicators and qualitative discussion of sustainability, which results in a value from 4 to 0, depending on if or if the components were not used in the environmental report. Using the arithmetic mean to calculate this scale was considered acceptable as a first approximation of the quality of sustainability reporting, since no detailed framework exists yet, which could provide appropriate weights for calculating a more refined index. CO_2 and NO_x are significant global pollutants (contributing e.g. to global warming) and Eco-balances are important management tools to holistically reduce a company's environmental impact. Finally, the use of a qualitative indicator of sustainability discussion addresses the fact that many sustainability aspects cannot be quantified easily.

reporting activities. One would expect that actual performance in terms of emission efficiencies is associated with the firms' environmental management and reporting quality.

Table 13: One-way ANOVA of the environmental report quality for the sectors studied

Sector	Mean length of environmental report	Mean 'sustainability reporting scale'	Mean length of environmental policy
Electricity	32.96 pages	2.50 points	24.89 lines
Pulp and Paper	25.33 pages	1.80 points	23.87 lines
Total	29.02 pages	2.14 points	24.36 lines
Significance of sector difference	Sig. = 0.032 F = 4.811 Df (total) = 57	Sig. = 0.003 F = 9.507 Df (total) = 57	Sig. = 0.796 F = 0.067 Df (total) = 57

As Table 13 shows, it was found that reports from the electricity sector are significantly longer (at 0.05 the level) and provide significantly more discussion of sustainability (at the 0.01 level) than in the paper sector. However, this is partly influenced by the fact that proportionally more reports in the paper sector are site-level statements, whereas comparatively more company-level reports have been received for the electricity sector (see the table on the characteristics of the data set in Chapter 6.2). The average length of the environmental policy was not significantly longer in the electricity sector than in the paper sector. This is, however, not surprising, given that the contents of an environmental policy are generic, rather than sector-specific (IRRC, 1996).

The average time emissions were reported backwards was also significantly longer in the electricity sector. In a second analysis a One-way ANOVA was carried out for the above indicators for the quality of the environmental reports and the two countries.

An ANOVA was also carried out for the above variables measuring the quality of the environmental reports to establish differences between two countries that were analysed.

Table 14: One-way ANOVA of environmental report quality for the countries studied

Country	Mean length of environmental report	Mean 'sustainability reporting scale'	Mean length of environmental policy
United Kingdom	30.46 pages	2.50 points	24.79 lines
Germany	28.24 pages	1.91 points	24.30 lines
Both countries	29.02 pages	2.14 points	24.36 lines
Significance of sector difference	Sig. = 0.632 F = 0.395 Df (total) = 57	Sig. = 0.025 F = 3.971 Df (total) = 57	Sig. = 0.851 F = 0.162 Df (total) = 57

Between countries, only the score on the sustainability rating scale differs significantly at the 0.05 level with the mean for the UK being significantly higher than for Germany. Thirdly, the quality of environmental reports was analysed with respect to the number of employees as a proxy variable for company size. However, no significant difference could be found for any of the three constitutive variables for the quality of environmental reports and the number of employees.

10. Testing of the Second Main Hypothesis

10.1 Introduction

The second hypothesis to be tested is whether a higher number of environmental performance indicators correlate at a significant level with a higher factual environmental performance of that company[15]. Within the methodological framework adopted, only the indirect effects of using several emission indicators on emission of pollutants other than those measured with the indicators can be assessed. The reason for this is, that if a firm does not use an indicator in the environmental report for a specific emission, then it is most likely, that these emissions are not reported at all (i.e. in the report, performance and indicator use are almost indistinguishable). However, as emissions (and hence environmental performance) have been normalised for production activity, they are to some extent de-coupled from indicator use. This justifies assessing air emissions (CO_2, SO_2, NO_x) against the use of a sum of three air emission indicators for these three emissions.

As described in Chapter 3, indicators are usually used within an overall performance measurement system, mostly in the form of an environmental management system that fulfils the requirements of the ISO 14001 or EMAS standards. Within the environmental management system, the system of environmental performance indicators is used for internal decision-making within the company regarding environmental issues, e.g. emission levels and reduction. As one production process is usually the source of not only one, but several emissions, several indi-

---

[15] The null hypothesis here is that there is no significant difference in environmental performance for different levels of use (i.e. numbers) for environmental performance indicators.

cators will need to be applied to this process to assess its overall environmental effects. If quantitative, physical indicators are used in this way within an overall measurement system that aims to minimise the total environmental effects of the production process in question, then the use of a set of indicators should simultaneously reduce several emissions. For example, identifying a process with high emission levels for one pollutant and medium-high levels for all others, using a set of EPIs should lead to substituting this process with a cleaner technology that likely also reduces the emissions of other pollutants. Therefore a higher number of indicators used in the overall performance measurement system could indirectly support reduced average emission levels of all pollutants. In this study, the assessment of indirect affects concentrates on the use of water indicators and water emissions in the pulp and paper sector.

In order to test the hypothesis that higher use of indicators corresponds with higher environmental performance, the correlation between the level of environmental performance and the number of indicators used has been calculated. However, to achieve a meaningful interpretation of the resulting correlation coefficients, it is necessary to first examine the scatterplots of the variables in question. This has to be done to ensure that there exists in fact a linear association between the variables, rather than no relationship at all or a non-linear relationship. This has been done and the results can be found in the Appendices I and II. Appendix I contains the scatterplots for three air emission variables from the data set (carbon dioxide, sulphur dioxide and nitrogenous oxide) for different firms against the sum of air emission indicators that were used by that firm. Diagrams 1, 3 and 5 show, respectively, scatterplots of carbon dioxide, sulphur dioxide and nitrogenous oxide emissions against a variable that describes the sum of all air emission indicators used in the environmental reports for the electricity sector only. The sum of air emission indicators could have a maximum value of 5 and consisted of carbon dioxide, carbon monoxide, sulphur dioxide, nitrogenous oxide and dust indicators. Diagrams 2, 4 and 6 of Appendix I show scatterplots for the same three air emission variables against a variable that describes the sum of these three air emissions (carbon dioxide, sulphur dioxide and nitrogenous oxide), only. These latter three diagrams are based on data for both sectors. Appendix II contains the scatterplots for six water emission variables and the sum indicator variable for water emissions in the Diagrams 1 to 6. The diagrams present scatterplots for the six water emissions chemical oxygen demand (COD), biological oxygen demand (BOD), nitrogen emissions (N), phosphorous emissions (P), emissions of adsorbable organic halogens (AOX) and water input, respectively. These emissions (which have an inverse relation to the level of environmental performance) were plotted against the sum of all water emission indicators used in the environmental reports for the paper sector only. The sum of these water emission indicators could have a maximum value of 7 and consisted of indicators for COD, BOD, N, P, AOX, the pH value (a measure of water acidity) and an indicator for total suspended solids (TSS). All plots in Appendix II are based on data for the pulp and paper sector, only. The diagrams of Appendix III are scatterplots of the air emission variables (carbon dioxide, sulphur dioxide and nitrogenous oxide) against the sum variable for water emission indicators. Analysing the scatterplots, it can be said that if at all there is a weak linear association between the number of indicators used in an environmental report and the level of air and water emissions, (which has an inverse relationship to environmental performance). Therefore the resulting correlation coefficients have to be interpreted rather cautiously.

10.2 Analysis for Air Emission and Indicators

For the relation between air emission variables and sum indicator variables significant correlation could only be found for nitrogenous oxide (NO_x) and carbon dioxide (CO_2), not for sulphur dioxide emissions. The results are summarised in the following Table 15.

Table 15: Significant correlation between air emissions and sum air indicator variables

Emission variable / Sum indicator variable	Nitrogenous oxide emissions per unit of output variable	Carbon dioxide emissions per unit of output variable
Sum air indicator variable 1 (CO_2, SO_2, NO_x, CO, Dust) - Electricity sector only -	No significant correlation	No significant correlation
Sum air indicator variable 2 (CO_2, SO_2, NO_x indicators) - Electricity sector only -	R = 0.466 Significant at 0.05 level (2-tailed)	No significant correlation
Sum air indicator variable 2 (CO_2, SO_2, NO_x indicators) - Data of both sectors -	R = 0.297 Significant at 0.05 level (2-tailed)	R=0.372 Significant at 0.01 level (2-tailed)

As can be seen from the table, there is a significant positive correlation between the number of indicators used in the environmental report and nitrogenous oxide emissions for the electricity sector alone as well as for both sectors together for the sum air indicator variable 2 (comprising of CO_2, SO_2, NO_x indicators). In the case of the electricity sector alone, the significant correlation could not be reproduced for the sum air indicator variable 1 (i.e. the sum of five air emission indicators) and should therefore be treated cautiously, as it could well be an artificial result. No significant correlation for either of the three air emission variables can be found for the sum air indicator variable 1 (comprising of the sum of CO_2, SO_2, NO_x, CO and Dust air emission indicators used in a firm's environmental report) for the electricity sector. Also in the case of carbon dioxide emissions, a significant positive correlation can be found with the sum air indicator variable 2 if data for both sectors together is used. However, as no significant correlation could be identified for the electricity sector on its own, this means that a very strong correlation between the sum air indicator variable 2 and carbon dioxide emissions exists only in the pulp and paper sector.

It was also found, that the three air emission indicators for carbon dioxide, sulphur dioxide and nitrogenous dioxide are used significantly more in the electricity sector than the pulp and paper sector (for the data of both countries). This might be due to the higher relevance of air emissions in the electricity sector. To ensure that the level of indicator use rather than other influences are responsible for the observed correlations (i.e. to assess multi-colinearity in the data set) correlation coefficients were calculated for several other variables of the data set. These are summarised in the following table:

Table 16: Correlation coefficients for several variables of the data set for both sectors

	ISO certification	EMAS verification	Number of employees	Country of company
Sector of company	R = -0.075 Not significant	R = -0.495 Sig. (0.01 level)	R = -0.126 Not significant	R = -0.353 Sig. (0.01 level)
Number of indicators used	R = -0.104 Not significant	R = 0.376 Sig. (0.01 level)	R = 0.248 Not significant	R = 0.450 Sig. (0.01 level)
Level of CO_2 emissions	R = -.433 Sig. (0.01 level)	R = 0.217 Not significant	R = -0.034 Not significant	R = 0.269 Sig. (0.05 level)
Level of SO_2 emissions	R = -0.217 Not significant	R = 0.378 Sig. (0.05) level	R = 0.008 Not significant	R = 0.335 Sig. (0.05 level)
Level of NO_x emissions	R = - 0.217 Not significant	R = 0.233 Not significant	R = 0.191 Not significant	R = 0.335 Sig. (0.05 level)

The significant correlations established in this table can be summarised as follows:

- All air emissions are significantly higher in the United Kingdom than in Germany.

- Companies in the UK use significantly more indicators than companies in Germany.

- There are significantly more electricity companies in the UK and correspondingly significantly more pulp and paper companies in Germany in the data set.

- Significantly more companies are verified under EMAS in the pulp and paper sector.

- EMAS-verified firms use significantly fewer indicators than firms not verified.

- Sulphur dioxide emissions of firms not verified under EMAS are significantly higher.

- Carbon dioxide emissions of firms certified under ISO are significantly higher than those for firms not certified under the ISO 1400x series standards.

The first result is consistent with the findings in the first part of the analysis, which highlighted the significant country differences. The second and third findings are related to the structure of the data set and essentially to the sampling strategy adopted for the survey.

The last three results are further discussed in the next section of the analysis on comparing the results for the two environmental management system standards (EMAS and ISO).

If the electricity sector alone is analysed in both countries the results broadly confirm the conclusions derived for both sectors together as can be seen from the following table (the number of indicators used now refers to the sum air indicator variable 1, i.e. the sum of the CO, CO_2, SO_2, NO_x and dust indicators).

The significant correlations established in this table can be summarised as follows:

- The SO_2 and NO_x air emissions are significantly higher in the United Kingdom than in Germany.

- Firms in the electricity sector in the United Kingdom have significantly higher number of employees, which is due to the sampling strategy adopted for gathering the data.

- Significantly more companies in the electricity sector are verified under EMAS in Germany compared to the UK which is again due to the adopted sampling strategy.

- Companies verified under EMAS have significantly lower numbers of employees and significantly lower SO_2 emissions than firms not verified under the EMAS standard.

- Correspondingly, firms certified under the ISO standard have significantly higher numbers of employees in the electricity sector, which is also due to the sampling strategy (in the UK the big electricity generators were sampled, which are mainly certified under ISO, whereas in Germany predominantly smaller generators were sampled which are usually certified under the EMAS standard).

Table 17: Correlations for several variables for the electricity sector in
         both countries

	ISO certification	EMAS verification	Number of employees	Country of company
Number of employees	R = -0.463 Sig. (0.05 level)	R = 0.611 Sig. (0.01 level)	R = 1.000 Not significant	R = 0.504 Sig. (0.05 level)
Number of indicators used	R = -0.064 Not significant	R = -0.051 Not significant	R = 0.049 Not significant	R = -0.233 Not significant
Level of CO_2 emissions	R = -0.135 Not significant	R = -0.241 Not significant	R = -0.191 Not significant	R = -0.200 Not significant
Level of SO_2 emissions	R = -0.184 Not significant	R = 0.464 Sig. (0.05) level	R = 0.056 Not significant	R = 0.494 Sig. (0.05 level)
Level of NO_x emissions	R = - 0.336 Not significant	R = 0.399 Not significant	R = 0.066 Not significant	R = 0.518 Sig. (0.01 level)

In summary, the established indicator-performance correlation for air emissions is inconclusive and might well be due to the structure of the sample i.e. the fact that most EMAS firms are located in Germany and usually use less indicators (which might be due to the fact that they are usually small firms spending less on environmental management).

10.3 Analysis for Water Emissions and Indicators

Concerning correlation for water emission variables and sum water indicator variables, only the pulp and paper sector could be analysed as only for this sector data was collected.

The only negative correlation between sum indicator variables and environmental performance variables for water emissions could be found for AOX emissions and water input. However only one of the six negative correlations identified proved to be significant at the 0.05 level. The significant correlations found for water emissions are listed in the following table.

Table 18: Significant correlation between water emissions & sum water indicator variables

Emission variable / Sum indicator variable	BOD per unit of output variable	Phosphor (P) emissions per unit of output variable	Water input per unit of output variable
Sum water variable 1 (Sum of COD, BOD, AOX, N, P, pH, TSS) - Paper sector only -	R = 0.544 Significant at 0.01 level (2-tailed)	R = 0.518 Significant at 0.05 level (2-tailed)	R = -0.396 Significant at 0.05 level (2-tailed)
Sum water variable 2 (Sum of COD, BOD, AOX, N, P indicators) - Paper sector only -	R = 0.497 Significant at 0.05 level (2-tailed)	R = 0.499 Significant at 0.05 level (2-tailed)	No significant correlation

As can be seen from the table, in the pulp and paper sector a significant positive correlation exists between the biological oxygen demand (BOD) per unit of output variable and both sum indicator variables for water indicators (i.e. sum water variable 1 and sum water variable 2). The same applies to the phosphor emissions per unit of output and the two sum indicator variables.[16] Surprisingly, in the light of all previous results, a significant negative correlation can be found between the water input per unit of output and the sum water variable 1 which represents the sum of seven possible indicators that are used in the environmental report of a firm. However, this is the only correlation at all that would support rejecting the second null hypothesis developed (that is, that a higher number of environmental performance indicators will not correlate at a significant level with a higher factual environmental performance of that company).

In order to ensure the assumed correspondence between the level of indicator use and emission levels, rather than other influences are responsible for the observed correlations (i.e. to assess multi-colinearity in the data set) correlation coefficients were calculated for several other variables of the data set in a similar way as above for the electricity sector together with a country-specific assessment of indicator-performance correlations. A single analysis for the UK was not possible in the paper sector, as the number of firms is too small (i.e. below or equal to seven firms). For the paper sector in Germany, significant correlations were found for the number of indicators used and the level of phosphorous emissions ($R = 0.550$) and for the level of indicator use and the level of water inputs ($R = -0.470$). Both results confirm the above analysis carried out for both countries together. With regard to other influences, the following significant correlations were identified:

---

[16] It has to be noted, that there is significant multi-colinearity between both sum indicator variables for water emissions as confirmed by the scatterplots in Appendix III as well as the corresponding correlation matrix.

- In the paper sector, the number of ISO certified companies is significantly higher in the UK than in Germany (which is due to the sample characteristics of the data set).

- Related to this, the number of EMAS verified companies is significantly higher in Germany, than in the UK (again, this is due to the sample characteristics).

- Firms surveyed in the paper sector are have a significantly higher number of employees in the UK, than in Germany (this is also due to the sample characteristics).

The results for the water sector indicate only small evidence for rejecting the null hypothesis that the actual environmental performance regarding water emissions of a firm in the pulp and paper sector is differing with different use levels for water emission indicators. The only variable supporting the results one would expect (i.e. that a higher number of indicators used will reduce emission levels and correspondingly improve environmental performance) was the level of water input in the paper sector.

In summary, the null hypothesis that a higher number of environmental performance indicators do not correlate at a significant level with a higher factual environmental performance of that company could not be rejected. (i.e. the null hypothesis that there is no difference in environmental performance could not be falsified). The results are even more counter-intuitive as they suggest rather the contrary of the original hypothesis: firms who have used a high number of indicators describing environmental performance in their reports have a rather low environmental performance. This has to be further discussed in the Chapters 8 and 9.

A possible way to confirm these findings for the second hypothesis developed in Chapter 5.1 could be a disaggregated analysis for the two environmental management system standards, EMAS and ISO. So far, the analysis indicates, that the number of indicators used by a firm (in its environmental report, but possibly also in internal decision-making processes) does not significantly correlate with a higher environmental performance. However, in the methodology applied here, only indirect influences of indicators measuring other emissions could be tested. The postulated existence of indirect influences is based on the assumption, that indicators are usually used for internal decision-making within EPI systems in the framework of environmental management systems as e.g. described in the EMAS and ISO standards.

Therefore another (indirect) way to test the relevance of environmental performance indicators could be an analysis of the two standards with regard to possible differences in the levels of environmental performance and use of indicators firms achieve. This is difficult however, as most firms in the study are either certified under the ISO standard or verified under the EMAS scheme and no comparison to firms whose environmental management systems are not audited to either standard is possible. Still, it might be possible to draw conclusions from the relative performance of firms under both standards by relating this information to the level of indicator use within the different standards.

11. EMAS, ISO, Environmental Performance and Quality of Reports

Given the rather undefined results for the relation between environmental performance and report quality, a very interesting question is how the environmental performance and the quality of environmental reports differs for firms certified under different environmental management system standard. The standards covered in the study were the EU-Eco Management and Audit Scheme (EMAS) and the international standard ISO 14001 (ISO). The following table describes the distribution of the different standards over the two sectors.

Table 19: EMAS and ISO certifications in each sector

	EMAS verification	ISO 14001 certification
Pulp and paper sector	83.3 %	36.4 %
Electricity sector	34.8 %	29.2 %

The results in this table are explained by the fact that some (especially bigger) pulp and paper firms are certified under both standards whereas some of the electricity firms (again especially bigger companies) are not certified to either standard as they have company standards that are broadly equivalent to international standards. In the case of the electricity sector, this allows a comparison of the performance between firms operating their environmental management system under no external standard at all, firms, which operate under the EMAS scheme, and firms, which operate under the ISO 14001 standard. For the paper sector, a comparison is only possible for firms operating under the EMAS scheme as opposed to those that are certified to the ISO 14001 standard.

Also most of the ISO-certified firms are based in the United Kingdom, whereas most of the EMAS-verified firms in the sample are from Germany as described in the following table:

Table 20: EMAS and ISO certifications in each country (% of total companies sampled)

	EMAS verification	ISO 14001 certification
United Kingdom	14.3 %	9.7 %
Germany	91.9 %	60 %

This imbalance is due to the differing recognition the two standards receive in the two countries. For the envisaged analysis, the country imbalance in the data set is rather problematic, as e.g. a high performance of EMAS verified firms can also be related to the fact that these firms are located in Germany. Vice versa for lower performance of ISO certified firms can be mainly due to the fact that they are predominantly located in the UK.

From the data analysis, a pattern emerges also for the relationship between ISO 14001 certification, EMAS verification, number of employees and whether the report was a site- or company-level one: ISO 14001 certified firms have a high number of employees as this certification is carried out at the company level whereas EMAS verified firms have lower numbers of employees as verification is site-based. The described correlation for EMAS verification and number of employees is significant at the 0.01 level (2-tailed). Also the correlation between ISO 14001 verification and number of employees is significant at the 0.05 level (2-tailed). As well the negative correlation between ISO 14001 certification and EMAS verification is significant at the 0.01 level (2-tailed). Also the correlation between a site-level report and EMAS verification is significant at the 0.01 level. Therefore a company that is verified under EMAS is most likely not certified under ISO, has a small number of employees and produces a site-level report. Analogously, a company certified under ISO 14001 is highly likely not verified under EMAS and has a high number of employees[17]. This is relevant for the results reported below, as consequently the non-EMAS firms are most likely ISO firms and vice versa, the non-ISO firms are most likely EMAS firms. However, as can be seen from the above two tables not every firm is necessarily certified under ISO or verified under EMAS.

In summary, the data set has the following characteristics regarding EMAS and ISO:

- Significantly more companies are verified under EMAS in the pulp and paper sector.

- Correspondingly, in the paper sector, the number of ISO certified companies is significantly higher in the UK than in Germany.

- The number of EMAS verified companies is significantly higher in Germany, than in the UK (for both sectors together).

- Significantly more companies in the electricity sector alone are verified under EMAS in Germany compared to the UK.

- Companies verified under EMAS have significantly lower numbers of employees.

- Correspondingly, firms certified under the ISO standard have significantly higher numbers of employees in the electricity sector.

---

[17] The correlation between reporting based on a company-level report and certification under the ISO 14001 standard was negative, though not significant.

An ANOVA was carried out regarding the correlation between three of constituent variables for report quality (i.e. length of report, length of environmental policy and score on the sustainability rating scale) with regard to certification of the company under ISO 14000. The result is summarised in Table 21:

Table 21: One-way ANOVA of the quality of environmental reports for ISO certification

Company certified under ISO 14001?	Mean length of environmental report	Mean 'sustainability reporting scale'	Mean length of environmental policy
Yes	28.00 pages	2.31 points	25.38 lines
No	28.37 pages	2.11 points	24.60 lines
Total	28.25 pages	2.18 points	24.8 lines
Significance of mean differences	Sig. = 0.925 F = 0.009	Sig. = 0.486 F = 0.492	Sig. = 0.871 F = 0.026

As can be seen, there are no significant differences between the mean values i.e. the quality of the environmental reports seems to be independent of a certification of a company under ISO and EMAS. With regard to the quality of environmental reports, an ANOVA was also carried out to identify possible correlation for sites with an environmental management system verified under EMAS. Table 22 summarises the results found:

Table 22: One-way ANOVA of environmental report quality for EMAS
verification

Company veri-fied under EMAS?	Mean length of environmental report	Mean 'sustainability reporting scale'	Mean length of environmental policy
Yes	25.06 pages	1.85 points	22.62 lines
No	36.26 pages	2.63 points	27.05 lines
Total	29.08 pages	2.13 points	24.21 lines
Significance of mean differences	Sig. = 0.005 F = 8.614	Sig. = 0.004 F = 9.263	Sig. = 0.298 F = 1.106

As the results show, verification of the site environmental management system under EMAS correlates significantly at the 0.01 level with lower values for the mean length of a report and the mean score on the 'sustainability reporting scale'. If however, the whole sample is considered (i.e. both, EMAS and ISO certified companies) then there is a linear relationship between the mean length of the environmental report and the mean length of the environmental policy. This can be seen from the scatterplot of both variables on the next pages. The linear relationship between these two variables also holds for both sectors separately as is also illustrated by the scatterplot.

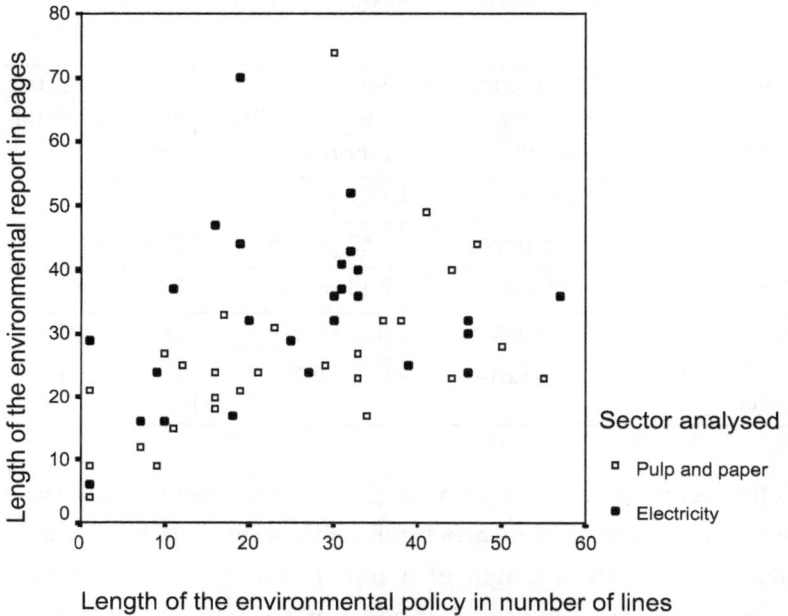

Figure 5: Scatterplot for relationship between length of report and the length of policy

Compared to the rather clear results for the actual environmental performance of firms, where the level of performance was clearly determined by country rather than by sector, the quality of environmental reports seems to have a more complex pattern of correlation. Given this, an analysis as to how air emission variables correlate with certification or verification under a certain standard should give valuable further insights.

Table 23: One-way ANOVA for the air emission variables and ISO 14001 certification

Company certified under ISO 14001?	Mean CO_2 emissions per unit	Mean SO_2 emissions per unit	Mean NO_x emissions per unit
Yes	714.31 t per unit	3.02 t per unit	1.13 t per unit
No	327.01 t per unit	1.43 t per unit	0.76 t per unit
Total	437.67 t per unit	1.91 t per unit	0.87 t per unit
Significance of Mean differences	Sig. = 0.002 F = 10.869	Sig. = 0.085 F = 3.109	Sig. = 0.148 F = 2.169

As can be seen from the table, companies not certified under ISO 14001 have significantly lower CO_2 and SO_2 emissions (at the 0.01 significance level) than those certified under this environmental management standard. This can be due to the fact that most of the companies not certified under ISO report under the EMAS scheme which would also be consistent with the results below for the relation between EMAS verification and environmental performance. In this case, the same analysis, applied to the variable 'EMAS verification' yields the following results:

Table 24: One-way ANOVA for the air emission variables and EMAS verification

Company verified under EMAS?	Mean CO_2 emissions per unit	Mean SO_2 emissions per unit	Mean NO_x emissions per unit
Yes	385.76 t per unit	0.94 t per unit	0.69 t per unit
No	584.08 t per unit	3.34 t per unit	1.07 t per unit
Total	462.66 t per unit	1.93 t per unit	0.85 t per unit
Significance of mean differences	Sig. = 0.134 F = 2.320	Sig. = 0.005 F = 8.85	Sig. = 0.116 F = 2.574

The results that sulphur dioxide emissions of firms verified under EMAS are significantly lower and that carbon dioxide emissions of firms certified under ISO are significantly higher than for the firms not certified (which are likely to report under the EMAS scheme) could indicate that EMAS produces higher environmental performance. This result has however to be interpreted cautiously, as most EMAS verified companies are located in Germany, and as well significant differences in emission levels do not apply homogeneously across both sectors. However, the additional fact that EMAS-verified firms use significantly less indicators than firms not verified might support the conclusion that the level of indicators used is less relevant for the level of environmental performance than the country location of a company.

12. Regression Analyses

After the previous chapters have given a more detailed picture of the factors influencing environmental performance of companies, it is now possible, based on the accumulated insights to formulate models for regression analysis. However, due to the small sample size, the results of such analyses can only give indicative results.

In a first regression, the factor scores derived from the factor analysis carried out for the air and water emissions in Chapter 8.3 were used as dependent variables. The independent variables in this regression were the total number of indicators used, country location and sector membership of the company, and the length of the environmental report. Also, whether an Eco-balance was used for data collection and whether a company was verified under EMAS or certified under ISO 14001 was entered as independent variables in the regression. The following table gives a model summary.

Regression analyses for these variables were carried out over the whole sample for the air emission factor score and for the water emission factor score in the paper sector, only.

In the first regression with the air emission factor score being the dependent variable all independent variables specified above are entered directly. The indicator variable used in this model is the total number of air emissions indicators out of three, which was recorded for both sectors, and the regression was consequently carried out across the whole sample, thereby pooling data from the two sectors.

Table 25: Model summary and ANOVA for regression for air factor
score (both sectors)

R	R Squared	Adjusted R Squared	Std. Error of the Estimate	Sum of Squares (Total)	df (Total/ Residual)	Mean Square (Regression)	F	Sig.
0.601	0.361	0.217	0.934	42.283	38/31	2.180	3.422	0.009

The most interesting result of this model is that only length of the environmental report and use of an Eco-balance for data collection have negative coefficients. This means, that the longer the environmental report is, the lower the emissions of a company or site are and that when a company uses an Eco-balance for data collection, this reduces emissions. Also, verification under EMAS or certification under ISO reduces emissions. Companies in Germany have lower emissions as well as have firms in the electricity sector. Companies which use more indicators in their reports can be expected to have higher emissions, which is in line with the more detailed findings on the correlation between environmental performance and the number of indicators used in Chapter 10.

These findings were confirmed by sensitivity analyses carried out by using the single air emissions (CO_2, SO_2 and NO_x) instead of the factor score as dependent variable and by adding further independent variables. This did not alter the results reported above except in the case of CO_2 emissions, where the coefficient for country location and ISO certification was negative.

In a second regression, the same model was calculated, this time using stepwise entry of variables in order to identify the best predictor. As dependent variable, the air emissions factor score and the separate air emissions were used. In the regression run with the air factor score as dependent variable, the result was that country location of a firm is the best predictor of the emission level. In the case of CO_2 emissions, certification under ISO was identified as the best predictor (which is in line with the results of the sensitivity analysis). In the regression run with SO_2 emissions as dependent variable, the best predictors were EMAS certification of a company and the length of the environmental report. For NO_x emissions, no model could be calculated. These results point to the need of using more than one predictor in order to forecast environmental performance of a company.

The second regression carried out used the water emission factor score as dependent variable, but used the total number of water emission indicators in the paper sector (out of seven) as independent variable for the number of indicators. Consequently, the analysis was carried out for the paper sector only, but still for both countries. The following table gives a model summary.

Table 26: Model summary and ANOVA for water factor score regression (paper sector)

R	R Squared	Adjusted R Squared	Std. Error of the Estimate	Sum of Squares (Total)	df (Total/ Residual)	Mean Square (Regression)	F	Sig.
0.869	0.755	0.673	0.611	18.239	16/12	3.441	9.231	0.001

The total number of water emission indicators used, the length of the environmental report and whether a company was certified under ISO

14001 all have positive coefficients. The only independent variable with a negative coefficient is whether an Eco-balance was used for data collection. Whether a company was verified under EMAS and country location of a firm were excluded as dependent variables. The regression coefficients for the number of indicators used, the length of the environmental report and whether an Eco-balance was used for data collection were found to be significant. When the number of years an emission is reported backwards on average is included, the adjusted R Square becomes 0.754 and this added independent variable has also a negative coefficient. The results mean that emissions can be expected to be lower if a company uses an Eco-balance, reports back for a long time its emissions or is certified under ISO 14001. Again it was found that the higher the number of indicators used by a firm the higher its emissions can be expected which is again in line with the results reported in Chapter 10. Interestingly, the result for the length of the environmental report differs for air and water emissions, which might point to a rather contingent relationship of this variable with environmental performance.

Using the stepwise entry method as described above a regression was then carried out with the water emissions factor score as dependent variable and the above independent variables. The four best predictors in the resulting model were (in sequence of their entry): the total number of water emission indicators used; whether an Eco-balance was used for data collection; the length of the environmental report and the number of years an emission was reported backwards. The model is summarised in the following table.

Table 27: Model summary and ANOVA for stepwise regression for water factor score

R	R Squared	Adjusted R Squared	Std. Error of the Estimate	Sum of Squares (Total)	df (Total/ Residual)	Mean Square (Regression)	F	Sig.
0.912	0.831	0.754	0.529	18.239	16/11	3.031	10.810	0.001

13. Summary of Results, Final Conclusions and Recommendations

13.1 Summary of Results

The objective of the first part of this book was to identify the extent of correlation between the physical environmental performance of a company, the use of quantitative physical environmental performance indicators and the quality of corporate environmental reporting of the company in two industrial sectors in two EU countries.

The basic research question therefore was, whether environmental reporting, the use of physical and quantitative environmental performance indicators and a company's actual environmental performance are positively correlated. To answer this general question correctly, two more specific null hypotheses were derived from this basic research question.

The first null hypothesis that the level of physical environmental performance does not significantly differ for different levels of quality of the environmental reports analysed could not be falsified i.e. rejected. The conclusion would be that a good or elaborate environmental report is not necessary guaranteeing a high level of environmental performance for that firm (see also Wagner (2004) and (2005c) on implications of this in the context of environmental management accounting and sustainable business).

The second null hypothesis that the level of physical environmental performance does not significantly differ for different levels of use of quantitative, physical environmental performance indicators (EPIs) could also not be falsified i.e. rejected. In all except of one case, the correlations for the indirect influence of indicators on other emissions were positive, leading to the rather contra-intuitive result that a higher number of indi-

cators used correlates with a lower i.e. worse environmental performance.

In order to assess the influence other factors have on the tested hypotheses and to provide a more precise description of variations in the underlying data set other possible influences were also analysed. These included e.g. the effects of industry sector and country membership, influences of country-specific environmental legislation and approaches to
environmental management and possible sectoral or national differences
in the use of physical indicators and the quality of environmental reports.

With regard to country differences it was found, that there is a much
stronger correlation for countries regarding the level of environmental
performance than for any of the other variables. All three air emissions
were on average significantly higher in the United Kingdom, than in
Germany.[18] The difference of emission levels between sectors was not
significant. This can point to a comparatively higher importance of sector-specific or general environmental legislation.

Some significant differences in report quality were found between sectors whereas almost no significant difference was found between the two
countries regarding the quality of environmental reports.[19] The level of
indicator use for air emissions is significantly higher for the UK. Therefore no evidence could be found for the claim that quantitative physical
environmental performance indicators are used more in Germany due to

---

[18] Due to an insufficient number of firms in the UK, a comparison was not possible
for water emissions.

[19] The variables measuring report quality were the length of the report, the length
of the environmental policy, the sustainability rating of the report and the number of years emissions were reported backwards.

a tradition in the application of Eco-balance analyses. However, it was found, that firms that use Eco-balances in their report have significantly lower air emissions.

Distinguishing between ISO certified and EMAS verified companies it was found that EMAS verified firms have slightly higher environmental performance and use slightly less environmental performance indicators. However, due to the structure of the data set, this can be explained by the fact that most EMAS verified firms are in the paper sector which uses comparatively lower numbers of indicators and that most of the EMAS verified companies (i.e. the firms in the paper sector) are located in Germany which has stricter environmental legislation.

13.2 Final Conclusions

Taken together, the results reported in Sections 10 and 12 suggest that voluntary schemes like environmental management schemes, if not designed properly, are less likely to achieve higher environmental performance than strict environmental legislation. It seems that companies do not manage what they measure, but rather measure what legislation requires. An analysis of economic instruments, a third possible environmental policy tool was not possible due to insufficient application and hence data. The general result that environmental legislation is likely to lead more reliably to higher environmental performance of a company than environmental management based on voluntary environmental management schemes is well in agreement with the conclusions of economic theory regarding the policy assessment of different environmental policy tools[20] (Endres, 1994).

---

[20] These are, broadly speaking, legislation, economic instruments and voluntary schemes (Endres, 1994).

This book so far aimed to assess the extent to which the level of environmental performance and the quality of environmental reports are consistent and consequently what credibility should be attributed to such reports. Although a relatively small sample size, inhomogeneities in the sample and partial violations of some assumptions underpinning the statistical analyses have to be acknowledged, various additional analyses were made to ensure that this would not seriously affect transferability and validity of the findings.

The results reported above also imply, that the use of a higher number of indicators or the production of an elaborate environmental report does likely not cause considerable improvements in the environmental performance of a company. Only the use of an Eco-balance seems to have a sizeable positive effect on environmental performance. The observed negative correlation between emission levels and the use of an Eco-balance as a tool for data gathering points to the possibility that the early stages of the environmental reporting process (i.e. those prior to calculation of specific indicators and the production of an environmental report) are more relevant for the levels of environmental performance firms ultimately achieve. It seems that a detailed data collection process (which is much supported by the use of an Eco-balance) and the resulting data base much assist the identification of optimisation potentials for improving environmental performance.

13.3 Recommendations

The higher quality of reports in the electricity sector (in both countries) can be explained by a higher exposure of the electricity sector to environmentalist pressure. Distinguishing between ISO certified and EMAS verified companies, it was found that EMAS verified firms have slightly higher environmental performance and use slightly less environmental performance indicators. However, due to the structure of the data set, this is likely explained by the fact that most EMAS verified firms are in the paper sector, which uses comparatively lower numbers of indicators and that most of the EMAS verified companies (i.e. the firms in the paper sector) are located in Germany which has stricter environmental legislation (Gordon, 1994; Handler, 1997; Scherer, 1997).

Taken together, the results firstly suggest that there is no strong association between the quality of corporate environmental reports and the actual environmental performance of firms. It needs to be noted that this is only assessed in terms of correlation, which can not necessarily be taken as proof of causation. However, the results imply that it would be rather speculative to assume that better environmental reporting causes better environmental performance, in which case it could be used as a valuable environmental management tool as well as a reliable proxy variable for external assessment of environmental performance given that reports usually address external audiences. It seems that companies do not measure what they can or want to manage from an environmental point of view, but rather measure what legislation requires.

Secondly, the findings also indicate, that environmental performance is significantly linked to country location (but not much to sector membership), whereas environmental report quality is more strongly linked to sector membership (but not much associated to country location). This possibly explains the fact that almost no significant association between these two aspects could be found. One interpretation of this is that environmental legislation, which is mainly country-related is a stronger driver of higher environmental performance, whereas environmental reporting is mainly rooted in voluntary environmental management schemes that tend to be more sector-related. This would also imply to some degree, that legislation is more important in achieving performance than voluntary schemes, a conclusion that is in agreement with recent empirical research on the effect of voluntary schemes on environmental performance (Tyteca *et al.*, 2002).

The results also imply that the use of a higher number of indicators or the production of detailed environmental reports are across whole industries unlikely to be related significantly to better environmental performance of companies. Only the reported use of an Eco-balance seems to be positively correlated with better environmental performance. The observed negative correlation between emissions efficiencies and the reported use of an Eco-balance as a tool for data gathering points to the possibility that the early stages of the environmental reporting process (i.e. those prior to calculation of specific indicators and the production of overall reports) are more relevant for the ultimate levels of environmental performance that firms achieve. It seems that a detailed data collection process (which is much supported by the use of an Eco-balance) and the resulting database assist much in the identification of optimisation potentials for improving environmental performance.

With regard to the legislation-competitiveness debate in environmental policy, more research seems to be necessary to identify the sector specific and time-dependent effects of legislation on a firm's competitiveness, assuming an increased importance of legislation as an environmental policy tool over voluntary schemes as indicated by this study. However, this has also to consider dynamic and inter-temporal aspects of both instruments: although the static efficiency of environmental legislation might be considerably higher than that of voluntary schemes, the dynamic efficiency of the latter might over-compensate this. This might be in the form of accelerating innovation processes towards cleaner technologies and clean production or by developing or opening up new technological trajectories. This issue seems to require further empirical analysis for both of the above sectors.

In the case of Eco-investment funds, country location of a company, or whether or not a firm uses an Eco-balance analysis to record its environmental effects might be a more reliable predictor for the environmental performance of a firm than other benchmarking criteria that are based on environmental management systems. This should also be analysed in more detail in future studies.

Finally with respect to the unavailability of results for the performance of economic instruments as an environmental policy tool, it seems necessary to monitor closely the emerging Eco-taxation schemes in several European countries and other economic instruments applied with regard to their efficiency in improving environmental performance.

Overall, this study indicates that consistency in environmental performance, use of EPIs and environmental reporting is rare, but future credibility of companies crucially depends on it. This points to the need of revising currently used standards for environmental management leading to more standardised indicators and data collection procedures (Ditz & Ranganathan, 1997). Revision should also aim for a life-cycle approach to environmental performance measurement and include the broader sustainability agenda, ultimately aiming for sustainability indicators (Wehrmeyer & Tyteca, 1998). This includes for example distribution issues on the firm level and employee participation (Cable, 1984). Recent developments in the chemical industry in this respect give hope that industry rises to the challenges of consistency and credibility (CEFIC, 1998).

The main conclusion of the first part of this book for its second part is that environmental reporting quality cannot be taken as a proxy variable for environmental performance. Therefore an analysis of the relationship between environmental and economic performance needs to apply physical environmental performance indicators to measure environmental performance directly, rather than using the quality of corporate environmental reports as a proxy variable. An important rationale for the second part of this book (which is to look closer at economic performance) is that relevant stakeholders (e.g. the financial sector or eco-investors) will in many cases only consider environmental performance (or its few correlates in corporate environmental reporting, such as eco-balances) relevant, if environmental performance is shown to correlate with economic performance. Ideally, such a correlation would be due to good environmental performance actually causing better economic performance, but this is difficult to test. The main linking element of the first and the second part of this book is the underlying data set, which is slightly expanded for the second part, particularly by including Dutch and Italian firms into the analysis. In doing so, the analysis becomes more European in scope, analysing the EU north to south, east to west.

14. An Empirical Analysis of the Relationship between Environmental and Economic Performance in the Paper and Electricity Industries

14.1 Introduction

The second part of this book looks in detail at the relationship between environmental and economic performance. From the first part of this book one has to conclude that environmental reporting quality cannot be taken as a proxy variable for environmental performance. Hence any analysis of the relationship needs to make use of environmental performance indicators to measure environmental performance directly. The second part of the book therefore, after formulating a theoretical model, reports results of an empirical analysis of two industrial sectors (paper manufacturing and electricity generation) for an enlarged data set of the first part of the book now covering four EU countries. The econometric analysis in the second part of the book uses new data to test hypotheses derived from the theoretical model and finds, for an emissions-based index in the paper manufacturing industry, a predominantly negative relationship, whereas for an inputs-based index no significant link is found. For the European electricity supply industry, the empirical analysis of an emissions-based index of environmental performance finds no significant relationship. Based on these results, the second part of the book arrives at the conclusion that for firms in environmentally-intensive industries, such as paper manufacturing and electricity generation, it is difficult to create a positive link between environmental and economic performance.

14.2 A Theoretical Model of the Relationship of Environmental and Economic Performance at the Firm Level

The objective of this research is to establish the relationship between the environmental performance and economic performance at the firm level in the European Union (EU), based on an analysis of companies in one specific industrial sector in four EU countries. This industrial sectors chosen for this analysis pulp and paper and electricity.[21] The countries in which firms in these sectors are analysed are Germany, Italy, the Netherlands and the United Kingdom of Great Britain[22]. The main research question addressed in the second part of this book is "What is the relationship between the environmental and economic performance of firms in specific industrial sectors and what is the influence of corporate environmental strategies on this relationship?". Corporate environmental strategies (CES) are distinguished here in terms of end-of-pipe and integrated pollution prevention strategies, based on actual physical environmental performance of companies. The hypothesis is that the relationship between environmental and economic performance of firms is either inversely U-shaped or negative in its functional form, and that CES may have some influence as well.

Characterized on the basis of quantitative indicators describing mass, energy and pollutant flows, environmental performance is linked to the

---

[21] The sector classification is based on the NACE code e.g. NACE 21.1 for pulp and paper manufacturing.

[22] Apart from the environmental relevance, the sectors and the four countries have been chosen because a high number of companies produce environmental reports or site-level environmental statements under EMAS in the two sectors in these countries. These are usually externally validated and guarantee sufficient availability of data. Additionally the paper and the electricity sector both produce fairly homogeneous products, which makes a comparison of physical environmental performance across firms in each sector possible.

economic performance of firms' by way of an in-depth statistical analysis using multiple regression analysis in general and panel data models in particular in order to address the above research question and to identify a possible relationship between the environmental and economic performance of firms. Based on the statistical analysis of a multiple-country data set of firms in two European manufacturing industries, the hypothesis derived from the question stated above, that the relationship between environmental and economic performance is either inversely U-shaped or negative in its functional form, can be tested. This hypothesis needs to take into account the influence of a number of important control variables. These variables are country membership, processes operated by firms, and firm size. The results of the analysis indicate that corporate environmental strategies (CES) may have an important influence as well.

Following the argument made by Schaltegger and Synnestvedt (2002) an inversely U-shaped curve would represent the "best" possible case for the relationship between environmental (and in a wider sense sustainability) and economic performance, since it allows for the existence of win-win situations with profitable environmental performance improvement activities (this is frequently referred to as the "revisionist view"). Alternatively, if environmental performance improvements can only increase costs and reduce profits for an individual firm, this would not be possible. Under such conditions (often termed the "traditionalist view"), the optimal level of environmental performance for a firm would be the one prescribed by environmental regulations, i.e. compliance without over-compliance. Figure 6 summarises these considerations in joining both relationships in one graphic representation and also shows the possibility of the relationship evolving over time due to innovation, as suggested by Porter (1991). This means, that over time, for a defined level of environmental performance, the maximum realisable level of economic performance will increase (see Schaltegger and Synnestvedt, 2002).

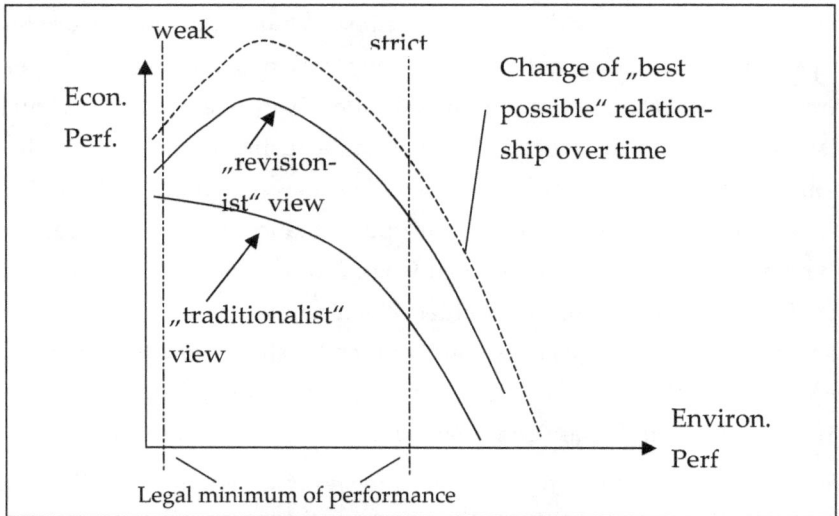

Figure 6:   Link of environmental and economic performance (Schaltegger, 1988; Lankoski, 2000; Wagner, 2000; Schaltegger &
Synnestvedt, 2002; Wagner, 2003a; 2003b; Wagner & Schaltegger, 2004a; 2004b; Wagner, 2005a; 2005b)

A novelty in this model e.g. not discussed by Schaltegger (1998) and Schaltegger and Synnestvedt (2002) or Lankoski (2000) is the question of how environmental regulation interacts with the model proposed in Figure 6. What becomes clear is that there are two distinct cases:

(i) The regulatory regime is "weak", so that the environmental perform-ance level required by regulation is below the optimum level of envi-ronmental performance according to the curve in Figure 6. In this case, under the "revisionist view" it would be beneficial (and thus rational for companies), to improve their environmental performance beyond the level required by law, since this would simultaneously improve their economic performance. Opposed to this under the "traditionalist" view, the optimum level of environmental performance would still be the one just achieving legal compliance with environmental and social regulation.

(ii) If the regulatory regime is "strict" (the right vertical line in Figure 6) then even under the "revisionist" view, the optimum level of environmental performance should not be higher than prescribed by regulatory compliance, as can be seen from the fact that the level of environmental performance which maximizes economic performance is lower than the minimum level of environmental performance, as required by environmental regulation. Since the same conclusions applies also to a "traditionalist view"-type curve, in this case the outcome for both types of curves would be the same, i.e. the optimal environmental performance level to chose is that which just achieves regulatory compliance.

In summary therefore, the analysis of the interaction of environmental regulation and the precise functional relationship between economic and environmental (and probably in a wider since also sustainability performance comprising both, environmental and social aspects) reveals that if regulation is weak then firms' rational choices depend crucially on whether the firm faces (or thinks it faces) a "revisionist view"-type or a "traditionalist view"-type relationship between economic and environmental/sustainability performance.

Based on different perceptions of a firm which relationship between economic and environmental/sustainability performance it faces and what the factual link is, four possible situations are possible as outcomes when regulation is "weak":

1. Firms are faced with a "traditionalist"-type relationship and also perceive so and regulation is weak. In this case firms will make the choice (based on their information and perception) of just being compliant with regulation which is also the optimal choice.

2. Firms are faced with a "traditionalist"-type relationship but perceive they are facing a "revisionist"-type relationship and regulation is weak. In this case firms will make the choice (based on their perception) of being over-compliant, which is not an optimal choice under the circumstances.

3. Firms are faced with a "revisionist"-type relationship and also perceive so and regulation is weak. In this case firms will make the choice (based on their perception) of being over-compliant which is also the optimal outcome.

4. Firms are faced with a "revisionist"-type relationship but perceive they face a "traditionalist"-type link and regulation is weak. In this case firms will make the choice (based on their information and perception) of just being compliant, which is not an optimal choice under the circumstances.

When regulation is "strict", firms will always chose to just be compliant regardless of whether the actual and perceived relationships differ or are the same. Given the possibility that firms cannot really establish which relationship they face, it seems thus in many cases to be rational to just be compliant, in particular if it is the case that improvements in economic performance from better environmental performance ("environmental profits") are comparatively small.

So far, a non-linear specification of the relationship between environmental and economic performance has neither been used in theoretical models, nor in empirical analyses. Testing for such a non-linear relationship will therefore be the focus of the remainder of this book. After briefly sketching out the basic research questions and hypotheses and the theoretical reasoning behind them, the next Chapter 15 reports the methodological aspects of the research. Subsequently results of the econometric analysis are presented in Chapters 16 and 17 and are discussed in detail. The final Chapter 18 draws conclusions and raises some policy issues.

15. Methodology of the Second Part

This section introduces the methodological approach adopted for the empirical analysis, used to test the hypothesis stated in Chapter 14 and theoretically justified in the previous section. The research design of the empirical analysis is a statistical design using purposive survey methodology. It includes a number of instruments (various EPIs and financial ratios), on which data was collected for subjects from two industrial sector). In the following, separate sections describe in detail (i) the subjects of this research, (ii) the instruments and measures used, (iii) the statistical analysis approaches and econometric specifications used in the empirical testing of the hypothesis formulated in Chapter 14 and (iv) the process data collection.

15.1 Subjects

The subjects of this research are firms from four European countries (Germany, Italy, the Netherlands and United Kingdom) in the pulp and paper manufacturing and electricity generation sectors (as defined by the 2-digit NACE code). The firms chosen were either single-site firms (i.e. sites) or firms with very few sites. This was done because the control of common system boundaries is easier for single-site firms and firms with few sites than for multi-site firms with many sites.[23]

Although the paper manufacturing and electricity sectors have different relative economic importance in the countries under observation, they both contribute in all countries to essential human needs. To improve e.g. environmental performance in the paper manufacturing sector

---

[23]   However, there are only very few multi-site firms in Europe and hence proceeding like this did not introduce a bias in the analysis.

whilst not deteriorating economic performance is therefore essential to ultimately achieve sustainable development and sustainability in this sector and thus a necessary condition for achieving in the industrial society as a whole. Behmanesh *et al.* (1993) find the paper sector to be consistently ranked fourth amongst all manufacturing industries with regard to its environmental impacts, which supports the environmental relevance of the paper manufacturing sector and the relevance of environmental aspects for firms' economic performance in this sector.

Regarding the choice of countries included in the first empirical analysis, data availability needed to be sufficient in both sectors as a whole, as well as in each individual country. These requirements could be met by choosing four European countries, namely Italy, the United Kingdom (UK), the Netherlands and Germany. In Germany as well as the in Netherlands, the extent of corporate environmental protection has achieved relatively high levels. However, in Germany command-and-control regulation is predominant, whereas in the Netherlands, a strong focus is on voluntary/negotiated instruments (e.g. negotiated industry agreements, so-called "covenants"). Generally, the economic relevance of the paper sector in all four countries chosen is very high, as can be seen from Table 28 below. Similar arguments also apply to the electricity generation industry in the four countries chosen.

Table 28: Number of pulp and paper mills and rank of the chosen countries

Country	Paper mills	Pulp mills	Rank paper	Rank pulp
United Kingdom	97	4	5th in EU	10th in EU
The Netherlands	25	2	10th in EU	12th in EU
Italy	210	15	1st in EU	7th in EU
Germany	198	20	2nd in EU	3rd in EU

(Source: CEPI, 1998)

Table 28 shows that with Italy and Germany, the countries with the two largest national paper manufacturing sectors in the EU are included in the data set. With the UK and the Netherlands, two further countries are included, in which the paper industry has relatively lower, yet still significant importance, as confirmed by their respective ranks.

15.2 Instruments and Measures

Quantitative measures of environmental and economic performance are particularly suited for an analysis of the relationship between environmental and economic performance for a number of reasons. Firstly, they can often be derived from publicly available information sources, such as financial reports or pollutant release and transfer registers (ER, TRI, CRI).

Secondly, quantitative indicators measure the outcomes of firms' environmental management activities and are thus more suited for a description of environmental and economic performance than effort measures (such as the amount of environmental management activities).

Thirdly, environmental performance indicators (i.e. normalised measures of environmental performance) and financial ratios have been used in several empirical studies to analyse the relationship between environmental and economic performance (e.g. Hart and Ahuja, 1996; Edwards, 1998; Johnson, 1996). Therefore, in the empirical analysis, no own instruments are developed, but well-established EPIs whose reliability and validity has been extensively tested (for example recently in the MEPI research project, see Berkhout *et al.*, 2001) are chosen. To proceed this way is often advocated over developing new instruments in the literature (Rudestam and Newton, 1992).

The variables used to operationalise the concept environmental performance are SO_2 emissions, NO_x emissions, COD emissions, total energy input, and total water input, all per tonne of paper produced. Olsthoorn *et al.* (2001) support the use of these indicators in the paper sector. Also, only for these variables used to operationalise environmental performance, data was sufficiently available to allow for meaningful analysis and results (in terms of not reducing too much the representativeness and thus generalisability of the results). Regarding the use of value added instead of physical production output (i.e. tonnes of paper produced) as denominator to normalise absolute environmental performance, there are theoretical arguments justifying the use of either of the two. Physical production output was used nevertheless, since the price of paper on the world markets dropped significantly between 1995 and 1996. It was assumed that this would influence more strongly value added than physical production output. In order to avoid distortions because of this, the latter was used as denominator. This choice is further supported by the high correlation of value added and physical production output in the data set. Similar reasoning was used in the electricity sector.

In order to use the above individual environmental performance indicators (all normalized to production output) in the regression analyses, three composite indices of these had to be calculated, using the method initially developed by Jaggi and Freedman (1992) in the adaptation used in Wagner *et al.* (2002) and Wagner (2005b) who also explain the precise method for index calculation. The indicators used to calculate scores for the first (outputs-oriented) index score were SO_2, NO_x (for the electricity and additionally COD for the paper sector). For the second (inputs-oriented) index score, total energy input and total water input were used. The reason for using two indices was firstly, that differentiation between input and output orientation allows assessment of methodological effects on the results. Secondly, the data was used more efficiently this way, since more cases could be included in the analysis. Thirdly, the input-oriented index reflects more to pollution prevention, whereas the output-oriented index reflects more end-of-pipe activities.

Broadly, economic performance can be subdivided into profitability (defined and measured in terms of accepted accounting-based measures), and in terms of longer-term competitiveness. Generally it is rather difficult to define and measure competitiveness, since it is more of a theoretical construct and since the factors that influence a firm's competitiveness change over time and are difficult to identify and measure before they manifest themselves in economic outcomes of the firm's operations in terms of its profitability, returns, market position and stock market valuation.

Given that economic performance in the short term can be approximately measured through profitability, the latter is measured in terms of operating profit financial ratios (esp. profitability/ efficiency ratios). Profitability ratios considered in the following are return on sales (ROS) and return on owners' capital employed (ROCE), and return on equity (ROE). These ratios have been used in studies in the U.S. and Europe (Hart and Ahuja, 1996; Edwards, 1998) to assess the relationship between environmental and economic performance and are therefore considered particularly valuable, partly because they allow (at least to some degree) a comparison between the results of studies for Europe and the United States. Since multi-colinearity between these ratios is high, they can only be used separately.

Next to the variables to be used to measure the concepts of environmental and economic performance, a number of economic control variables were included in this research in the regressions with economic performance as dependent variable. These are the asset-turnover ratio, the gearing ratio/debt-to-equity ratio, firm size and the square of firm size, and country dummy variables. The use of the square of firm size addresses potential non-linearities and this variable is often used in applied econometric work (e.g. Wagner, 1998). Finally, a sub-sector classification was developed for the paper and electricity sectors, on the basis of which sub-sector dummy variables were defined and included into the regression equations. Use of the asset-turnover ratio has been suggested by Russo and Fouts (1997) and by Schaltegger and Figge (1998) to control for differences in capital intensity. Hart and Ahuja (1996) suggest inclusion of the debt-to-equity ratio to control for differences in capital structure. The debt-to-equity ratio is calculated in this research as the inverse of the solvency ratio, less than one (i.e. debt-to-equity ratio = (1/solvency ratio) − 1). The solvency ratio is defined as the ratio of shareholder funds to total assets. Next to the variables described above to measure the concepts of environmental and economic performance respectively, and the sector dummy variables accounting for the sub-sectors firms are operating in, country dummy variables for the four countries in which data was collected for paper manufacturing firms, as well as a variable measuring the size of firms (in thousands of employees) were used as variables in the empirical analysis of this research. Table 29 lists all variables used in empirical analysis of the research. The precise definitions of economic and control variables, as provided in Table 29, are according to Belzer (2000).

Table 29: Summary of variable definitions for all variables used in the analysis

Concept	Variable	Description	Type[24]
Economic performance	ROCE	Return on capital employed [%], defined as: (pre-tax profit + interest paid) / (shareholders' funds + non-current liabilities)*100	continuous (cont.)
	ROE	Return on equity [%], defined as: pre-tax profit (loss) / shareholders' funds*100	cont.
	ROS	Return on sales [%], defined as: pre-tax profit (loss) / operating revenue * 100	cont.

---

[24] In the table, cont. and dum. refer to continuous (interval/ratio scale) type and dummy type variables, respectively.

Environmental performance	COD	Emission of chemical oxygen demand per output in [kt/t] or in [kt/kWh]	cont.
	SO₂	Emission of sulphur dioxide [kt/t] or [kt/kWh]	cont.
	NOₓ	Emission of nitrogenous oxides [kt/t] or [kt/kWh]	cont.
	Water / energy input	Total water input per unit of output [1000 litres/t] and total energy input per unit of output[kWh/t], respectively	cont.
Control variables in regression analyses	debt-to-equity ratio	Inverse of solvency ratio minus one [solvency ratio measured in %, defined as: shareholders' funds/ total assets*100	cont.
	asset turnover ratio	Inverse of turnover-to-asset ratio, i.e. asset turnover ratio [GBP/GBP], defined as: total assets per operating revenue	cont.
Country	United Kingdom	Firm located in the United Kingdom	dummy (dum.)
	Italy	Firm located in Italy	dum.
	Netherlands	Firm located in the Netherlands	dum.
	Germany	Firm located in Germany (reference group)	dum.

Subsectors (paper industry)	Indus-trial	Packaging corrugated/other boards	dum.
	Cultural	Newsprint, magazine-grade, graphics fine paper (reference group)	dum.
	Mixed	Cultural and industrial paper production combined	dum.
	Other	Other paper production	dum.
Sub-ectors (electricity industry)	Mixed	Mixed fossil (coal, oil) and nuclear fuel inputs	dum.
	Mixed fossil	Mixed fossil fuel inputs e.g. coal, oil (reference group)	dum.
	Other	Other fuel input (renewable energy sources, e.g. wind energy, pure nuclear fuel, pure gas as fuel input)	dum.
Other	Firm size	Number of employees (thousands)	cont.

15.3 Econometric Specifications

The analysis of the empirical relationship of environmental and economic performance of firms involves an estimation procedure which is based on a panel data model in which environmental and economic performance are considered to be in a causal relationship, i.e. the indicators used to measure environmental performance are considered to influence the economic performance variables which are the endogenous variables. For the analysis, a pooled model based on Ordinary Least Squares (OLS) regression and ignoring the panel structure, a random effects panel data model and a fixed effects panel data model are used. The specification of these models is presented in the following (Kohler and Kreuter, 2001; Johnston and DiNardo, 1997). The pooled model ignores the panel structure of the data and is estimated using OLS regression. It has the specification:

$$y_{it} = \alpha + \mathbf{x}_{it}\beta + \mathbf{z}_i\gamma + u_{it} \qquad (1)$$

where i = 1 .. N units under observation; and t = 1 .. T time periods for which data is collected. In this specification, y_{it} denotes the observation on the dependent variable (economic performance) for a firm i in a period t. x_{it} represents the set of time-variant independent variables (i.e. regressors), and z_i the time-invariant explanatory variables.

The errors u_{it} here are assumed to be identically and independently distributed (iid) i.e. the observations are assumed to be serially uncorrelated across individuals and time and the errors are assumed to be homoscedastic, and the assumptions of the classical linear model are met. Hence, OLS is the efficient estimation method.

However, ignoring the panel structure of the data can be problematic for two reasons (Johnston and DiNardo, 1997). Firstly, because even though the pooled model yields consistent estimates of the regression coefficients, standard errors will be under- and significance levels hence be overstated. Secondly, compared to Generalised Least Squares (GLS) regression, the use of OLS as estimation method does not result in efficient estimates of the regression coefficients. To address these problems, two well-established models, the random and the fixed effect models exist. The difference between the fixed effects and the random effects model is based on whether the time-invariant effects are correlated with the regressors (which is the case for the fixed effects) or (in case of the random effects model) not. For the random effects model for panel data, the specification is (variables as in (1) above):

$$y_{it} = \alpha + x_{it}\beta + z_i\gamma + u_{it} \tag{2}$$

with
$$u_{it} = \mu_i + \varepsilon_{it} \tag{3}$$

In (3), u_{it} is composed of the disturbance μ_i reflecting left-out variables that are considered time-persistent (in the sense that for each firm i, these remain broadly the same over time) and the idiosyncratic error ε_{it}.[25] In the random effects model, the individual effect μ_i is assumed to be uncorrelated with the time-variant independent variables x_{it}. The estimation method for the random effects model is GLS, which is efficient (Johnston and DiNardo, 1997, p. 391).

For the fixed effects model, other than the random effects model, the assumption is that the individual effect μ_i is correlated with the time-variant independent variables x_{it}. This means that although the basic

---

[25] More precisely, in the random effects model, the disturbance is a random variable, which is however constant for each observation on one specific firm. This means that observations of one specific firm are considered to be more similar, than observations of different firms (Johnston and DiNardo 1997; Kohler and Kreuter 2001).

specification given in (2) and (3) remains, the interpretation differs, in that the disturbance μ_i is a constant (and thus represented by a dummy variable) for each unit of analysis, i.e. here for each specific firm. The fact that the disturbance is a constant in the fixed effects model implies that all time-invariant variables will be dropped during the estimation. The reason for this is, that technically all time-invariant variables (which are also represented by dummy variables) are fully multi-colinear with the (constant) disturbance (Kohler and Kreuter, 2001; Johnston and DiNardo, 1997, p. 397). Intuitively, this means that a change in the dependent variable for a specific unit of analysis for which observations exist cannot be attributed to a time-invariant variable, i.e. it cannot be said, which of the time-invariant variables has caused which part of the change observed in the dependent variable (Kohler and Kreuter, 2001). To decide, which of the two models (random or fixed effects) is more approriate, the Wu-Hausman test is used. If the test is significant, then the null hypothesis that there is no significant difference between the estimation results for both models is rejected. Assuming that the model is correctly specified, this implies that the fixed effects model is more appropriate, i.e. it results in consistent and efficient estimates, whilst the estimates in the random effects model are inconsistent. However, if the null hypothesis is not rejected, implying that the random effects model is valid, the fixed effects model still leads to consistent (but in this case inefficient) estimates of the identifiable parameters, which here are the time-variant variables (Johnston and DiNardo, 1997, pp. 402-403).

To also test for the existence of random effects (in cases, where the Wu-Hausman test turns out to be insignificant), the Breusch-Pagan test, which is a Lagrangian Multiplier test, is additionally carried out. If the test statistic of the Breusch-Pagan test is significant, this confirms the existence of random effects. If it is insignificant, then in cases, where also the Wu-Hausman test is insignificant, conclusions can be drawn on the basis of the pooled model estimated with OLS (StataCorp, 1997).

16. Results of the Analysis in the European Paper Industry

16.1 Introduction

For testing for the correctness of the theoretical model in the paper manufacturing industry, the panel regression framework described above and incomplete panel data on a set of 37 paper firms in four EU countries (Germany, Italy, Netherlands and United Kingdom) over the period from 1995 to 1997 were used. Table 30 provides an overview of the coverage of the paper sector as a whole in each country for the years 1996 and 1997. For 1995, data on the total production capacity, which was necessary for the assessment of coverage, was not available.

As can be seen from Table 30, percentage coverage changes little in each country from 1996 to 1997 due to the already mentioned even distribution of firms across countries and periods. Coverage is best in the Netherlands (approx. 37-38%) and worst in Italy (approx.7-9%). However this is also due to the fact that Italy has much larger total production capacity than the Netherlands. Also, it is necessary to take into consideration that total figures for each country are based on production capacity, not actual production. Thus, the figures are a conservative estimate of coverage. Given, that production is always smaller or equal to capacity, coverage may well be better than suggested by coverage figures.

Table 30: Overall coverage of the paper sector in the countries (based on annual production)

	Covered by sample 1995	Total 1995	Covered by sample 1996	Total 1996	Coverage 1996	Covered by sample 1997	Total 1997	Coverage 1997
Germany	3,775.3	N/a	3,589.17	15,890.0	0.226	3,984.90	16,893.0	0.236
Italy	561.471	N/a	579.199	7,850.00	0.074	801.695	8,415.00	0.095
Netherlands	1,208.1	N/a	1,211.60	3,266.00	0.371	1,275.00	3,316.00	0.384
United Kingdom	1,445.2	N/a	1,424.48	6,812.00	0.209	1,586.92	6,798.00	0.233
All Countries	6,990.1	N/a	6,804.45	33,818.0	0.201	7,648.52	35,422.0	0.216
Countries overall		N/a	33,818.0	79,115.0	0.427	35,422.0	87,408.0	0.405

Sources: Own calculations for individual countries, CEPI (1998) for country totals; All values in kt; Country totals refer to production capacity, not actual annual production

The remainder of this section reports the results found when empirically evaluating the relationship between environmental and economic performance in the European paper industry based on the statistical procedures introduced above (random effects (RE) and fixed effects (FE) panel regressions and OLS regressions). The research hypothesis was tested for two specifications of the environmental performance index during the empirical analysis. Results based on the panel regression framework described in the previous chapter are reported in the following.

16.2 Results for the Output-Oriented Environmental Performance Index

This section reports results for the output-oriented environmental performance index using the panel regression framework described. In addition to the variables provided in Table 29, the squares of firm size and the respective environmental performance index were added in the regression in order to account for non-linearities in the relationship. The results for the pooled data and the RE and FE models for economic performance indicators are reported separately in Tables 31 to 33 for the three measures of economic performance used: return on capital employed (ROCE), return on sales (ROS) and return on equity (ROE). Also the results of the Breusch-Pagan Lagrangian Multiplier and the Wu-Hausman specification tests are reported. As can be seen for ROCE, as dependent variable used to measure economic performance, the model with fixed effects is the best specification, since the Wu-Hausman test is significant. The FE model is also overall significant, and the hypothesis, that no fixed effects exist for any firm (i.e. that all u_i are equal to zero) is also rejected. In the model, the linear term of the environmental index is significant (at the 1% level) and has positive effect on ROCE. In addition to that, the squared term of the environmental index with a significance of 10.4% is also almost significant (at the 10% level) and has a negative effect on ROCE. The result is also economically relevant, since a 10% increase of environmental performance increases ROCE by 33.02 units, all else being equal (the high increase is due to the environmental index taking values between zero and one).

Table 31: Estimation for ROCE as dependent variable
(output-based index)

Model type	Pooled Model		RE Model		FE Model	
Independent variable	Coef.	Std.Err.	Coef.	Std.Err.	Coef.	Std.Err.
Environmental index	0.9413	1.8787	2.6506	2.5800	*33.0213*	8.4538
Square of env. index	-0.9618	1.8805	-2.6762	2.5923	-135.91	81.1471
Firm size	0.1486	0.1130	0.1513	0.1475	0.3435	0.2946
Square of firm size	-0.0273	0.0266	-0.0257	0.3508	-0.0443	0.0682
Leverage	0.0200	0.0174	0.0005	0.0221	-0.0523	0.0336
Asset turnover ratio	-0.0276	0.0311	-0.0306	0.0347	-0.0188	0.0406
Other sub-sector	**0.3380**	0.1429	*0.3398*	0.1863	-	-
Industrial sub-sector	-0.0250	0.0772	0.0002	0.1030	-	-
Mixed sub-sector	0.0035	0.0638	0.0202	0.0868	-	-
United Kingdom	**0.1901**	0.0753	*0.1829*	0.1014	-	-
Italy	0.1570	0.1235	0.1379	0.1611	-	-
Netherlands	0.0885	0.0833	0.0520	0.1162	-	-
Constant	-0.0996	0.1144	-0.0695	0.1491	13.6172	10.7321

No. of observations	63	63	63
R-squared	0.1857	0.1494	0.4310
F statistic	0.95		*4.04*
Wald χ^2		7.03	
F statistic (all $u_i = 0$)			*2.23*
Breusch-Pagan test		0.42	
Hausman test (χ^2)			*24.94*

Bold and italic figures refer to significance at the 5% and 10% levels, respectively. Figures that are bold and italicised at the same time refer to significance at the 1% level.

Also the squared term is economically relevant. Firm size and its square, leverage, as well as the asset turnover ratio have no significant effect on ROCE. The level of environmental performance which maximises ROCE in the FE model is equal to an index value of 0.12. With the index taking values between zero and one, this corresponds to a relatively low level of environmental performance.

Concerning ROS as measure of firms' economic performance, Table 32 below that the fixed effects specification is most appropriate (as signified by the significant Wu-Hausman test and rejection of the hypothesis that all individual effects u_i are simultaneously equal to zero). Results indicate that the linear term of the environmental performance index has a positive but insignificant effect on ROS whilst the squared term of the index has a significant and negative effect, which is also relevant in economic terms: a 10% increase of environmental performance reduces ROS by 7.2%, all else being equal. The level of environmental performance, which maximises ROS in the fixed effects model corresponds to an index value of 0.0188. Since the index takes only values between zero and one, this corresponds to a very low level of environmental performance, which is consistent with the observation that only a significant and increasingly negative effect of environmental on economic performance exists for ROS. Firm size and its square have no significant effect on ROS as dependent variable. However, leverage was found to have a significant negative effect on ROS (1% level), whereas the asset turnover ratio was found to be insignificant in the fixed effects model.

Table 32: Estimation for ROS as dependent variable (output-based index)

Model type	Pooled Model		RE Model		FE Model	
Independent variable	Coef.	Std.Err.	Coef.	Std.Err.	Coef.	Std.Err.
Environmental index	-0.0674	0.7138	0.1024	1.0904	2.7342	2.8037
Square of env. index	0.0563	0.7159	-0.1129	1.1000	**-71.661**	27.0024
Firm size	*0.0726*	0.0422	0.0609	0.0575	0.0781	0.0979
Square of firm size	-0.0117	0.0101	-0.0085	0.0140	-0.0123	0.0227
Leverage	**-0.0140**	0.0062	***-0.0221***	0.0073	***-0.0272***	0.0093
Asset turnover ratio	***0.0341***	0.0116	0.0151	0.0116	0.0149	0.0134
Other sub-sector	0.0563	0.0350	0.0408	0.0549	-	-
Industrial sub-sector	-0.0139	0.0275	-0.0087	0.0395	-	-
Mixed sub-sector	-0.0341	0.0249	-0.0274	0.0380	-	-
United Kingdom	**0.0599**	0.0281	*0.0699*	0.0421	-	-

	Coef.	Std.Err.	Coef.	Std.Err.	Coef.	Std.Err.
Italy	0.0483	0.0476	0.0455	0.0669	-	-
Netherlands	*0.0562*	0.0309	0.0517	0.0478	-	-
Constant	-0.0285	0.0419	0.0165	0.0575	**8.7277**	3.3084
No. of observations	68		68		68	
R-squared	0.4399		0.3803		0.3114	
F statistic	**3.60**				**2.64**	
Wald χ^2			*20.85*			
F statistic (all $u_i = 0$)					**3.66**	
Breusch-Pagan test			**5.89**			
Hausman test (χ^2)					**15.49**	

Bold and italic figures refer to significance at the 5% and 10% levels, respectively. Figures that are both bold and italicised refer to significance at the 1% level.

Table 33: Estimation for ROE as dependent variable (output-based index)

Model type	Pooled Model		RE Model		FE Model	
Independent variable	Coef.	Std.Err.	Coef.	Std.Err.	Coef.	Std.Err.
Environmental index	1.3953	2.6383	2.7703	3.7803	15.9770	10.5930
Square of env. index	-1.4857	2.6459	-2.8397	3.8100	**-226.09**	102.0207
Firm size	0.2446	0.1559	0.2332	0.2063	0.4814	0.03700
Square of firm size	-0.0378	0.0374	0.0304	0.0501	-0.0726	0.0858
Leverage	0.0048	0.0231	**-0.0541**	0.0274	***-0.1505***	0.0352

Asset turnover ratio	-0.0148	0.0430	-0.0409	0.0448	-0.0177	0.0508
Other sub-sector	0.2067	0.1293	0.1760	0.1871	-	-
Industrial sub-sector	-0.0800	0.1015	0.0063	0.1372	-	-
Mixed sub-sector	-0.0398	0.0921	0.0029	0.1304	-	-
United Kingdom	0.1501	0.1039	0.1344	0.1449	-	-
Italy	0.2280	0.1758	0.1825	0.2332	-	-
Netherlands	0.1010	0.1142	0.0087	0.1648	-	-
Constant	-0.1196	0.1547	0.0470	0.2041	**26.5516**	**12.4999**
No. of observations	68		68		68	
R-squared	0.1650		0.0957		0.4662	
F statistic	0.91				*5.10*	
Wald χ^2			11.00			
F statistic (all $u_i = 0$)					*3.45*	
Breusch-Pagan test			2.28			
Hausman test (χ^2)					*33.40*	

Bold and italic figures refer to significance at the 5% and 10% levels, respectively. Figures that are both bold and italicised refer to significance at the 1% level.

For the estimations with ROE as dependent variable, Table 33 shows similar findings as were made for ROS. Here again, fixed effects were found to be the most appropriate model. As for ROS, the linear term of the index has a positive, yet insignificant, effect on ROE. Opposed to this, the squared term has a significant negative effect on ROE, with the ROE-maximising level of environmental performance corresponding to an index value of 0.0353. This effect is also relevant in economic terms, since a 10% increase in environmental performance reduces ROE by 22.6%, all else being equal. Compared to this the significant negative effect of leverage is relatively small in terms of economic magnitude. As for ROS, leverage was found to have a significant negative effect on ROE in the FE model.

16.3 Results for the Input-Oriented Environmental Performance Index

This section reports results for the input-based environmental performance index, again using the panel regression framework described earlier. As for the output-based index, in addition to the variables provided in Table 29, the squares of firm size and the respective environmental performance index were added in the regression in order to account for non-linearities in the relationship. The results for the pooled, the RE and the FE models for are reported in Tables 34 to 36, respectively and also the results of the Breusch-Pagan Lagrangian Multiplier and Hausman specification tests are provided.

As can be seen from Table 34 for ROCE as dependent variable used to measure economic performance, the model with RE is the best specification, since the Hausman test is insignificant (i.e. the fixed effects model is not better than the random effects model in that the estimated coefficients are not significantly different between the two models). Even though the Breusch-Pagan test is insignificant, i.e. it does not reject the null hypothesis that the variance of the u_i equals zero for all i, the random effects model is still preferred over the pooled model, since the former is overall significant, but the latter not. In the model, the linear term of the environmental index, as well as its squared term are insignificant. Also, firm size and its square, leverage, as well as most dummy variables have no significant effect on ROCE. Only the asset turnover ratio has a significant negative (at the 10% level) and the dummy variable for the UK has a significant positive effect on ROCE (at the 5% level) in the RE model as well as in the OLS model. However, the OLS model is overall insignificant. The effect of the asset turnover ratio is relatively small in economic terms. A unit increase in the asset turnover ratio would only decrease ROCE by 0.05%, all else being equal (since ROCE is measured in percent). The effect of a firm being located in the UK increases ROCE by 0.23%, relative to the case of a firm being located in Germany, all else being equal.

Table 34: Estimation for ROCE as dependent variable (input-based index)

Model type	Pooled Model		RE Model		FE Model	
Independent variable	Coef.	Std.Err.	Coef.	Std.Err.	Coef.	Std.Err.
Environmental index	-0.7853	1.4843	-0.7853	1.4843	-9.293	34.6386
Square of env. index	2.2771	2.6960	2.2771	2.6960	28.5100	352.7174
Firm size	0.0437	0.1078	0.0437	0.1079	0.1503	0.4495
Square of firm size	-0.0056	0.0256	-0.0056	0.0256	-0.0267	0.0915
Leverage	0.0208	0.0136	0.0208	0.0136	-0.0067	0.0319
Asset turnover ratio	-0.0470	0.0274	-0.0470	0.0274	-0.1093	0.1047

Other sub-sector	-0.1160	0.1066	-0.1160	0.1066	-	-
Industrial sub-sector	-0.1267	0.7255	-0.0127	0.0725	-	-
Mixed sub-sector	-0.0259	0.0656	-0.0259	0.0656	-	-
United Kingdom	**0.2256**	0.0883	**0.2256**	0.0883	-	-
Italy	0.1207	0.0826	0.1209	0.0826	-	-
Netherlands	0.0540	0.0787	0.0540	0.0787	-	-
Constant	0.0356	0.1186	0.0356	0.1186	0.3707	2.0381
No. of observations	55		55		55	
R-squared	0.3113		0.3113		0.0826	
F statistic	1.58				0.36	
Wald χ^2			18.99			
F statistic (all $u_i = 0$)					0.58	
Breusch-Pagan test			1.34			
Hausman test (χ^2)					1.49	

Bold and italic figures refer to significance at the 5% and 10% levels, respectively. Figures that are bold and italicised at the same time refer to significance at the 1% level.

Concerning ROS, the results indicate that the pooled model is most appropriate, since the Breusch-Pagan test is insignificant and since only the pooled model is overall significant. In the pooled model, the linear and the squared term for the environmental performance index are insignificant, as are the linear and the squared term of firm size, i.e. firm size has no significant effect on economic performance measured in terms of ROS. Both, leverage, as well as the asset turnover ratio have a significant negative effect on ROS at the 10% and 1% levels, respectively, in the pooled data model.

Concerning sub-sector dummy variables (with the "Cultural" sub-sector being used as the reference group), the dummy for the "Mixed" sub-sector has a significant negative effect (10% level) in the pooled model on ROS. Regarding country dummy variables (with Germany being used as the reference group), United Kingdom, Italy and the Netherlands were found to be significant and positive in the pooled regressions for ROS at the 1%, 10% and 5% levels, respectively. However, for Italy and the Netherlands, the significant effects in the pooled model become insignificant in the random effects model. Only the positive effect of the United Kingdom (compared to Germany) dummy remains significant at the 5% level.

Table 35: Estimation results for ROS as dependent variable
(input-based index)

MODEL TYPE	Pooled Model		RE Model		FE Model	
Independent variable	Coef.	Std.Err.	Coef.	Std.Err.	Coef.	Std.Err.
Environmental index	0.3741	0.5207	0.4179	0.6436	-9.8877	9.3986
Square of env. index	-0.7689	0.9664	-0.8542	1.1789	75.8150	98.3765
Firm size	0.0616	0.0396	0.0498	0.0531	-0.0155	0.1271

Square of firm size	-0.0084	0.0094	-0.0055	0.0128	-0.0011	0.0258
Leverage	*-0.0097*	0.0049	*-0.0105*	0.0057	-0.0101	0.0090
Asset turnover ratio	***-0.0279***	0.0099	-0.0137	0.0115	-0.0366	0.0278
Other sub-sector	-0.0044	0.0280	-0.0031	0.0433	-	-
Industrial sub-sector	0.0016	0.0250	-0.0205	0.0350	-	-
Mixed sub-sector	*-0.0412*	0.0237	-0.0318	0.0339	-	-
United Kingdom	***0.0873***	0.0304	**0.0898**	0.0444	-	-
Italy	*0.0601*	0.0302	0.0586	0.0425	-	-
Netherlands	**0.0731**	0.0281	0.0530	0.0402	-	-
Constant	-0.0498	0.0431	-0.0299	0.0575	-0.1023	.5305
No. of observations	59		59		59	
R-squared	0.4578		0.4181		0.0951	
F statistic	*3.24*				0.46	
Wald χ^2			15.02			
F statistic (all $u_i = 0$)					*1.69*	
Breusch-Pagan test			0.17			
Hausman test (χ^2)					6.92	

Bold and italic figures refer to significance at the 5% and 10% levels, respectively. Figures that are bold and italicised at the same time refer to significance at the 1% level.

In terms of economic relevance, for ROS as dependent variable, leverage has a relatively small influence only, since a unit increase in leverage would only result in a 0.01% decrease of ROS, all else being equal, whereas a unit increase of the asset turnover ratio would result in an almost 0.03% decrease of ROS. Sector membership in the "Mixed" sub-sector reduces ROS by 0.04%, compared to membership in the "Cultural" sub-sector. Compared to these effects, country membership is more relevant in economic terms, since location in Italy, the Netherlands or the UK increases ROS by between 0.06% to 0.09%, relative to Germany.

Table 36: Estimation results for ROE as dependent variable (input-based index)

Model type	Pooled Model		RE Model		FE Model	
Independent variable	Coef.	Std.Err.	Coef.	Std.Err.	Coef.	Std.Err.
Environmental index	-0.9554	1.6794	-0.7280	1.8663	-34.871	32.6102
Square of env. index	1.4652	3.1169	0.9647	3.4336	241.249	341.3374
Firm size	0.0631	0.1277	0.0659	0.1525	-0.0332	0.4408
Square of firm size	0.0037	0.0303	0.0036	0.0366	-0.0136	0.0897
Leverage	0.0013	0.0157	-0.0084	0.0174	-0.0341	0.0312
Asset turnover ratio	-0.0333	0.0321	-0.0500	0.0355	**-0.2089**	0.0965
Other sub-sector	-0.0298	0.0902	-0.0304	0.1169	-	-
Industrial sub-sector	-0.0110	0.0808	0.0169	0.0979	-	-

Mixed sub-sector	-0.1141	0.0766	-0.1070	0.0941	-	-
United Kingdom	**0.2064**	0.0980	*0.2073*	0.1222	-	-
Italy	0.1562	0.0974	0.1756	0.1185	-	-
Netherlands	0.0782	0.0908	0.0347	0.1116	-	-
Constant	0.0581	0.1391	0.0904	0.1637	-0.0697	1.8406
No. of observations	59		59		59	
R-squared	0.2564		0.2424		0.2108	
F statistic	1.32				1.16	
Wald χ^2			11.85			
F statistic (all $u_i = 0$)					1.32	
Breusch-Pagan test			0.04			
Hausman test (χ^2)					5.09	

Bold and italic figures refer to significance at the 5% and 10% levels, respectively. Figures that are bold and italicised at the same time refer to significance at the 1% level.

Concerning the model with ROE as dependent variable reported in Table 36, none of the models estimated is overall significant, nor are the Hausman and Breusch-Pagan tests. Since the pooled and the random effects models do not differ qualitatively, results are reported for these two, given that they are the most suitable ones in the absence of fixed effects (i.e. the hypothesis that all u_i are simultaneously equal to zero could not be rejected). In both, the pooled and the random effects models, both, the linear and squared terms of the environmental performance index and of firm size were found to be insignificant, as were firm size and its square. In fact, the only significant independent variable was the dummy for firms located in the United Kingdom. This dummy was positive and had a significant effect at the 5% level in the pooled and at the 10% level in the random effects (RE) model. In terms of economic relevance, location of a firm in the UK increased ROE by 0.21%, relative to a firm being located in Germany. Whilst this is a relative moderate increase in absolute terms, it is still approximately two to three times higher than the effect observed in the case of ROS. Therefore, the effect is also somewhat relevant in economic terms, at least in a comparative perspective with the other measures of economic performance. All other independent variables in the pooled and random effects models were found to be insignificant.

17. Results of the Analysis in the European Electricity Industry

17.1 Introduction

The variables used to operationalise the concept environmental performance in the electricity generation industry are mainly (but not exclusively) SO_2 emissions, NO_x emissions, CO_2 emissions, all per kWh electricity produced the use of which is supported in the electricity supply industry.[26] Physical production output (in kWh) was used as a denominator to normalize data.

A sub-sector classification was developed for the electricity supply industry depending on the main fuel input of each company, on the basis of which sub-sector dummy variables were defined and included in the regression equations to control for fuel input differences. Table 37 lists those variables used in empirical analysis which differ compared to the paper manufacturing industry.

For testing the research question using the panel regression framework described above, incomplete panel data was used on a set of 17 to 19 firms (depending on the year in question) in the electricity supply industry of four EU countries (Germany, Italy, Netherlands and United Kingdom) over the period from 1995 to 1997.

---

[26] Olsthoorn *et al.* (2001) provide detailed arguments why the use of these indicators is appropriate.

Table 37: Summary of variable definitions differing in the electricity
industry from definitions for the pulp and paper industry

Concept	Variable	Description	Type[27]
Environ-mental perfor-mance	CO_2	Carbon dioxide emission per unit of output [kt/kWh]	cont.
	SO_2	Emission of sulphur dioxide per unit of output [t/kWh]	cont.
	NO_x	Emission of nitrogenous oxides per output[kt/kWh]	cont.
	Index	Environmental index based on SO_2 and NO_x	cont.
	Square of index	Square of environmental index based on SO_2 and NO_x	cont.
Sub-sector	Mixed	Mixed fossil (coal, oil) and nuclear fuel inputs	dum.
	Mixed fossil	Mixed fossil fuel inputs e.g. coal, oil (reference group)	dum.
	Other	Other fuel input (renewable energy sources, e.g. wind energy, pure nuclear fuel, pure gas as fuel input)	dum.

Table 38 provides an overview of the data for firms in 1996 and 1997, including data on environmental management system (EMS) certification

---

[27] In the table, cont./dum. refer to continuous (interval/ratio scale) type and dummy type variables, respectively.

status. Data for 1995 does not differ much since the same firms are included, only some do not have data available for all years.

Based on a separation of firms in those with a certified EMS and those without, for a number of environmental performance variables (CO_2 emissions, SO_2 emissions, NO_x emissions, total waste, hazardous waste, municipal waste, recycled waste, BOD emissions, COD emissions, total fuel/coal input, self-generated electricity, and water input all transformed to relative indicators using electricity production), it was tested (separately for 1996 and 1997) if significant differences between the two groups exist. The same was done for a number of economic variables (number of employees, sales, return on sales (ROS), return on equity (ROE), return on capital employed (ROCE), the current ratio and the solvency ratio).

Table 38: Overview of firms included in the data analysis for 1996 and 1997 and EMS status

Country Year	1996: ISO 14001	1996: EMAS	1997: ISO 14001	1997: EMAS
Germany	0 of 9	2 of 9	0 of 8	2 of 8
Italy	0 of 2	0 of 2	0 of 2	1 of 2
Netherlands	0 of 2	0 of 2	0 of 1	0 of 1
United Kingdom	1 of 6	0 of 6	2 of 6	0 of 6
Total	1 of 19	2 of 19	2 of 17	3 of 17

No significant differences were found for any of the environmental performance variables listed in Tables 29 and 37. Significant differences for firms with/without EMS (based on non-parametric Mann-Whitney tests) were only found for the solvency ratio in 1997 based on whether or not firms were EMS-certified in 1997, i.e. using non-time lagged category variables (U=8, W=74, Z=-1.828, 10% level (2-tailed), n=15). No significant differences were found for time-lagged influences of EMS certification on economic performance. Even though the data base for year-by-year analyses is somewhat limited in the data set, these findings cast some doubt on the benefits from adoption of a certified EMS (either EMAS or ISO 14001-based) by firms. It seems that certification of a site or firm to an environmental management systems standard by itself neither signals environmental excellence, nor economic success in the European electricity generation industry.

17.2 Empirical Analysis of the Relationship in the Electricity Industry

This section reports the results found when empirically evaluating the relationship between environmental and economic performance in the European electricity generation industry based on the statistical procedures introduced in Chapter 15.3 (random effects (RE) and fixed effects (FE) panel regressions and OLS regressions). The research hypothesis was tested using an environmental performance index based on SO_2 and NO_x emissions per kWh during the empirical analysis. Results based on the panel regression framework described in the previous section are reported in the following.

In addition to the variables provided in Tables 29 and 37, the squares of firm size and the environmental performance index were added in the regression in order to account for non-linearity in the relationship. The results for the pooled data and the RE and FE models for economic performance indicators are reported separately in Tables 39 to 41 for the three measures of economic performance used: return on capital employed (ROCE), return on sales (ROS) and return on equity (ROE). Also the results of the Breusch-Pagan Lagrangian Multiplier and the Wu-Hausman specification tests are reported.

As can be seen for ROCE, as dependent variable used to measure economic performance, the model with random effects is the best specification, since the Wu-Hausman test is insignificant, while the Breusch-Pagan test is significant. The RE model is also overall significant, and the hypothesis, that no fixed effects exist for any firm (i.e. that all u_i are equal to zero) is also not rejected. In the RE model, neither the linear, nor the squared term of the environmental index have a significant effect on ROCE.

The RE model and the pooled model do almost not differ in their results. The only exception is the influence of leverage on ROCE, which is almost significant in the pooled model and becomes significant (at the 10% level) in the RE model, having a negative effect on ROCE.[28] Also a country influence of UK location is significant and economically relevant, indicating that UK-located firms have a significant higher ROCE than firms located in Germany (which is the reference group).

Next to these significant influences, only the membership in the industry sub-sector using mixed inputs of fossil and nuclear fuels (i.e. firms that operate fossil as well as nuclear power plants) has a significant (at the 10% level) but economically (compared to UK location of a firm) not very strong positive influence on ROCE.

---

[28] This illustrates very clearly the effect of not taking into account the panel structure of the data used.

Table 39: Estimation for ROCE as dependent variable in the electricity industry

Model type	Pooled Model		RE Model		FE Model	
Independent variable	Coef.	Std.Err.	Coef.	Std.Err.	Coef.	Std.Err.
Environmental index	0.1012	0.2315	0.1012	0.2315	0.4313	128.4738
Square of env. index	-0.0850	0.2483	-0.0850	0.2483	-0.3003	80.6821
Firm size	0.0024	0.0022	0.0024	0.0022	0.0072	0.0153
Square of firm size	-0.0000	0.00002	-0.0000	0.00002	-0.0001	0.0003
Leverage	-0.0157	0.0094	*-0.0157*	0.0094	*-0.0681*	0.0341
Asset turnover ratio	0.0104	0.0137	0.0104	0.0137	*-0.0929*	0.0447
Other fuel based plant	0.0562	0.0447	0.0562	0.0447	-	-
Fossil & nuclear	0.0430	0.0238	0.0430	0.0238	-	-
United Kingdom	*0.1648*	0.0228	*0.1648*	0.0228	-	-
Italy	-0.0012	0.0503	-0.0012	0.0503	-	-
Netherlands	0.0576	0.0450	0.0576	0.0450	-	-
Constant	0.0291	0.0369	0.0291	0.0369	0.1152	2.1458
No. of observations	45		45		45	
R-squared	0.7280		0.7280		0.2470	
F statistic	*8.03*				1.09	

Wald χ^2		*88.34*
F statistic (all $u_i = 0$)		0.65
Breusch-Pagan test		*2.94*
Wu-Hausman test		4.88

Bold and italic figures refer to significance at the 5% and 10% levels, respectively. Figures that are bold and italicised at the same time refer to significance at the 1% level.

Concerning ROS as measure of firms' economic performance, it was found (Table 40) that the pooled model is most appropriate (as signified by the insignificant Wu-Hausman and Breusch-Pagan tests which indicate, that neither the random effects, nor the fixed effects models are a better specification than the OLS model). Results indicate that neither the linear nor the squared term of the environmental performance index have any significant effect on ROS. The country location of a firm and its plants in the UK has a significant positive effect on ROS, relative to country location in Germany, which is also relevant in economic terms: location in the UK increases ROS by 10%, all else being equal. Next to country location, the asset turnover ratio has also a significant positive effect on ROS, which is however less significant than country membership, since a unit increase in the asset turnover ratio results only in a 2% increase of ROS. Firm size and its square have no significant effect on ROS as dependent variable, and the same is the case for leverage. Also, none of the dummy variables for different fuel sources have any significant effect on ROS. Findings are therefore quite similar to those for

ROCE, where also environmental performance did not have an influence on economic performance.

Table 40: Estimation for ROS as dependent variable in the electricity industry

Model type	Pooled Model		RE Model		FE Model	
Independent variable	Coef.	Std.Err.	Coef.	Std.Err.	Coef.	Std.Err.
Environmental index	0.0054	0.2433	0.0162	0.2335	28.4665	107.1274
Square of env. index	-0.0211	0.2632	-0.0289	0.2288	-17.9	67.2766
Firm size	0.0027	0.0020	0.0024	0.0028	-0.0016	0.0127
Square of firm size	-0.0000	0.00002	-0.0000	0.00003	0.00009	0.0003
Leverage	-0.0014	0.0069	-0.0066	0.0095	-0.0279	0.0277
Asset turnover ratio	**0.0262**	0.0128	**0.0378**	0.0163	*0.1164*	0.0373
Other fuel based plant	0.0276	0.0470	0.0436	0.0600	-	-
Fossil & nuclear	0.0192	0.0249	0.0335	0.0354	-	-
United Kingdom	*0.1090*	0.0205	*0.1105*	0.0293	-	-
Italy	0.0352	0.0530	0.0093	0.0635	-	-
Netherlands	-0.0244	0.0413	-0.0149	0.0555	-	-
Constant	-0.0052	0.0288	0.0164	0.0384	-0.4715	1.6113
No. of observations	50		50		50	

R-squared	0.5473	0.5358	0.3393
F statistic	*4.18*		1.97
Wald χ^2		**24.44**	
F statistic (all $u_i = 0$)			*1.81*
Breusch-Pagan test		0.31	
Wu-Hausman test			7.36

Bold and italic figures refer to significance at the 5% and 10% levels, respectively. Figures that are bold and italicised at the same time refer to significance at the 1% level.

Table 41: Estimation for ROE as dependent variable in the electricity industry

Model type	Pooled Model		RE Model		FE Model	
Independent variable	Coef.	Std.Err.	Coef.	Std.Err.	Coef.	Std.Err.
Environmental index	-0.112	0.5359	-0.1115	0.5359	36.7482	294.7007
Square of env. index	0.0414	0.5798	0.0414	0.5798	-23.116	185.0734
Firm size	0.0005	0.0043	0.0005	0.0043	-0.0051	0.0350
Square of firm size	-0.000	0.00005	-0.00001	0.00005	0.00007	0.0007
Leverage	**0.0373**	0.0151	**0.0373**	0.0151	0.0047	0.0763

Asset turnover ratio	-0.016	0.0282	-0.0161	0.0282	0.2103	0.1027
Other fuel based plant	0.0105	0.1035	0.0105	0.1035	-	-
Fossil & nuclear	0.0557	0.0547	0.0557	0.0547	-	-
United Kingdom	*0.1744*	0.0451	*0.1744*	0.0451	-	-
Italy	0.0198	0.1168	0.0198	0.1168	-	-
Netherlands	-0.152	0.0911	*-0.1521*	0.0911	-	-
Constant	0.0657	0.0634	-0.1196	0.1547	-0.6797	4.4327
No. of observations	50		50		50	
R-squared	0.4949		0.4949		0.1913	
F statistic	*3.38*				0.91	
Wald χ^2			*37.23*			
F statistic (all $u_i = 0$)					0.75	
Breusch-Pagan test			3.24			
Wu-Hausman test					6.18	

Bold and italic figures refer to significance at the 5% and 10% levels, respectively. Figures that are bold and italicised at the same time refer to significance at the 1% level.

For the estimations with ROE as dependent variable, as reported in Table 41, similar findings were made as for ROS and ROCE in that again environmental performance has no significant effect on economic performance. For ROE, random effects were found to be the most appropriate model. As for ROS, UK location of a firm has a positive and significant effect on ROE. Location in the Netherlands has a significant negative effect on ROE. Other than this, only leverage has a small but significant positive effect on ROS. Results remained largely unchanged, when time-lagged independent variables were used, and when the time-lagged dependent variable was included on the right-hand side of the regression equation as an explanatory variable.

18. Overall Findings, Interpretations and Recommendations

Based on the results presented in the previous sections, the significant coefficients in the panel regressions models are now discussed with regard to the implications they have for the relationship between environmental and economic performance. Overall, for the paper manufacturing industry, the results confirm the inversely U-shaped relationship between environmental and economic performance formulated at the beginning of the book for the output-oriented environmental performance index in the fixed effects models. The positive part of the relationship was however found to be relatively weak. For the input-oriented environmental performance index, where the pooled models are most appropriate, no significant relationship could be detected.

For the electricity generation industry, the results do not support any significant relationship between environmental and economic performance, as proposed at the beginning of the paper. This finding does not alter, when the specification of the regression model is changed to using time-lagged independent variables, i.e. assessing a time-lagged effect of the independent variables on the dependent variable. Also, results do not change, when the dependent variable is included as an explanatory factor on the right-hand side of the regression equation (e.g. ROCE in period t+1 is explained by the explanatory variables set out in Table 1 and ROCE in period t, and equivalently for ROS and ROE). Most coefficients found to be significant remain so even when changing the specification of the regression equation as described.

The results found in the paper industry for financial leverage in terms of the debt-to-equity ratio in the most appropriate models (fixed effects for the output-oriented index and the pooled model for the input-oriented index) do not show a very clear pattern. Generally, the non-significance of leverage in the case of ROCE for both indices is in-line with theoretical reasoning, since theoretically ROCE in the way it is calculated should not be affected by capital structure. This increases the confidence, which can be put into the basic model specification in terms of the dependent and independent variables.

In the electricity generation industry, the results found for financial leverage in terms of the debt-to-equity ratio in the most appropriate models (random effects for ROCE and ROE, and the pooled model for ROS) do not show a very clear pattern: leverage has a significant negative effect on ROCE, no significant effect on ROS and a significant positive effect on ROE.

Otherwise, the results in both sectors seem to reflect (at least to some degree) the underlying theoretical debate about the influence of gearing on firms' costs of capital. Hay and Morris (1991) suggest at least five different phases in thinking about leverage and its effect on firm's capital costs and profitability. Their analysis suggests that it is very difficult to meaningfully interpret the coefficient of the debt-to-equity ratio beyond its function as a control variable in the regression analyses reported in this book. Therefore the gearing/debt-to-equity ratio, as well as the asset turnover ratio (for which similar arguments hold) should be understood as necessary control variables in regression models with economic performance as dependent variable, without which equations may be misspecified and, as a result, estimates may be biased.

Firm size has no significant influence on the three economic performance variables in the relevant models (regardless of the type of environmental index) of the empirical analysis in both industry sectors analysed. This provides very strong evidence that as far as the effect of firm size on economic performance is concerned, no significant effect exists at the level of one individual industry sector.

Concerning sub-sector dummies in the paper industry sample, in the estimations with the environmental index based on energy and water inputs, the "Mixed" sub-sector dummy variable has a significant negative effect at the 10% level on ROS. For all other estimations with the index based on energy and water inputs, the coefficients for the sub-sector dummy variables were found to be insignificant. Also, sub-sector dummies were insignificant for all equations with the outputs-oriented environmental performance index based on COD, NO_x and SO_2, except for a significant negative effect (at the 5% level) of the dummy variable for the "Other" sub-sector on ROCE in the pooled model. However, here the pooled model was inferior to the fixed effects model. Therefore there is remarkable homogeneity in the results of the first empirical analysis in that of the sub-sector dummies included in the models (when focusing on the most appropriate specification for each estimation) only the "Mixed" sub-sector has on one occasion only a significant effect on economic performance, which is negative. This seems to indicate, that sub-sector influences are likely of lesser relevance.

A negative coefficient for the "Mixed" sub-sector dummy means that firms in this sub-sector have lower returns on sales than firms in the "Cultural" sub-sector, all other things being equal. In order to interpret this effect it has to be remembered, that the "Mixed" sub-sector was defined as including those firms, which produce at least two types of paper of the three basic types cultural papers, industrial papers and other papers (e.g. tissue). The basic technological unit of a paper firm (and in this sense a better measure of production technology then the proxies used here based on sub-sector classification) is the individual paper machine.

One paper machine can only produce one type of paper in the short term. Therefore, firms in the "Mixed" sub-sector must have at least two different paper machines producing at least two different types of papers. This observation can be the basis for explaining why firms in the "Mixed" sub-sector have significantly worse economic performance than firms operating in one highly profitable sub-sector. Another argument here is that the use of different production technologies only allows lower production outputs and therefore does not allow benefiting from economies of scale which are significant in the paper manufacturing industry (Zavatta 1993).

Concerning sub-sector dummies in the electricity generation industry in the estimations for ROCE, the dummy variable for the mixed "Fossil & nuclear plant" sub-sector had a significant positive effect at the 10% level on ROCE in that membership of a firm in this sector increased ROCE by around 4%. For all other estimations, the coefficients for the sub-sector dummy variables were found to be insignificant. Therefore there is also remarkable homogeneity in the results of the second empirical analysis in that of the sub-sector dummies included in the models (when focusing on the most appropriate specification for each estimation) only the mixed "Fossil & nuclear plant" sub-sector had on one occasion a significant effect on economic performance. This seems to indicate, that sub-sector influences are likely of lesser relevance for the electricity industry.

A positive coefficient for the mixed "Fossil & nuclear plant" sub-sector dummy means that firms in this sub-sector have lower returns on capital employed, all other things being equal, than firms in the "Mixed fossil fuel inputs" sub-sector (e.g. combining coal and oil-fired power stations) which was the reference group. In order to interpret this effect it has to be remembered, that the "Fossil & nuclear plant" sub-sector was defined as including those firms, which generate electricity from a mix of fossil-fired and nuclear-fuelled power stations. Therefore, firms in this sub-sector may take advantage of a better cost situation of nuclear power stations, as compared to pure fossil fuel-based power stations. This may explain why firms in the "Fossil & nuclear plant" sub-sector have significantly better economic performance than firms operating in a purely fossil fuel-based sub-sector of the electricity supply industry.

As a result of the findings for the country dummy variables in the paper industry sample in the models estimated in the Chapter 16, it can be concluded, that if there is a significant difference, then firms located in the United Kingdom perform better relative to firms located in Germany. For ROS and the input-based index, also firms located in Italy and the Netherlands perform relatively better than firms located in Germany in the relevant model (pooled model).

For the electricity generation industry, as a result of the findings for the country dummy variables in the models estimated in Chapter 17 of this book, it can be concluded, that if there is a significant difference, then firms located in the United Kingdom perform better relative to firms located in Germany. This is an effect, which is significant for all three dependent variables used and is thus the most strongly supported stylized fact emerging from this research.[29] One very likely explanation of this result is the difference in the degree of liberalization of the electricity industry. In the UK, for the whole observation period, the electricity supply industry was highly deregulated, whereas for Germany, for the period of 1995-1997 the sector consisted of a number of regional monopo-

---

[29] For ROE, firms located in the Netherlands perform relatively worse than firms in Germany in the relevant model (random effects). Since this effect is not found for ROCE and ROS it is however less persistent in the data.

lies.[30] Whilst a regional monopoly is likely leading to higher price levels in the market, it also enables firms to add a margin on top of their production cost in order to finance any investments or capital outlays. Firms operating in a regional monopoly setting therefore do not require meeting capital market requirements in order to have sufficient access to external sources for financing. Opposed to this, in a liberalized market such as the UK market, firms require access to external financing sources in order to fund investment or expansion plans, since in a liberalized market no protection against competitors exists any more. Because of this, market prices depend on the action of all firms active in the market which makes it impossible for firms to set prices beyond the equilibrium price and thus highly unlikely to finance all investments through pricing. This in turn makes it necessary for firms to access capital markets which impose certain requirements in terms of profitability. This is a likely explanation for the significant positive effect of UK country location on the economic performance of firms. This significant country effect also indicates that market settings (especially whether or not a market is deregulated) are a comparatively stronger influence factor on economic performance than is environmental performance. This in turn raises the question, whether in liberalized electricity markets, drivers exist for firms to voluntarily improve their environmental performance, or whether an increased pressure on firms to improve their financial and economic performance will actually deteriorate their environmental performance, given that there seems to be no link of the latter to economic or financial performance. This issue should be addressed in more detail in future research.

---

[30] See Berkhout *et al.* (2001), Graichen (2002), BMWi (2001) for details of the different market structures of European energy markets at the national level.

From the comparative analysis of the relationship between environmental and economic performance in two environmentally-intensive industry sectors in Europe, the picture emerges, that market settings (i.e. external factors) as well as strategy considerations (i.e. internal factors) both can have an effect on the relationship, but that situational aspects determine which of these dominates. From the results it is concluded that for firms in the paper industry which are oriented towards pollution prevention, the relationship between environmental and economic performance is better than for those with more of an end-of-pipe orientation, yet still not significantly positive but, as it seems, in the best case insignificant. Nevertheless, there seems to be some influence of firm-internal strategy choice on the relationship in the paper industry. Opposed to this, in the European electricity generation industry, there seems to be a comparatively stronger influence of firm-external factors such as market parameters. This may indicate, that the electricity industry still operates more under the structure-conduct-performance (SCP) theorem of traditional industrial economics, whereas in the paper industry, the model of the active firm developed more recently in industrial organization as a counterpart to the SCP theorem is more appropriate. Further research could aim at analyzing in more detail if this interpretation holds and in particular, what the strategic consequences of this would be for firms.

19. Appendices

Appendix I: Scatterplots for testing possible linear associations between air emissions and air emission indicator variables

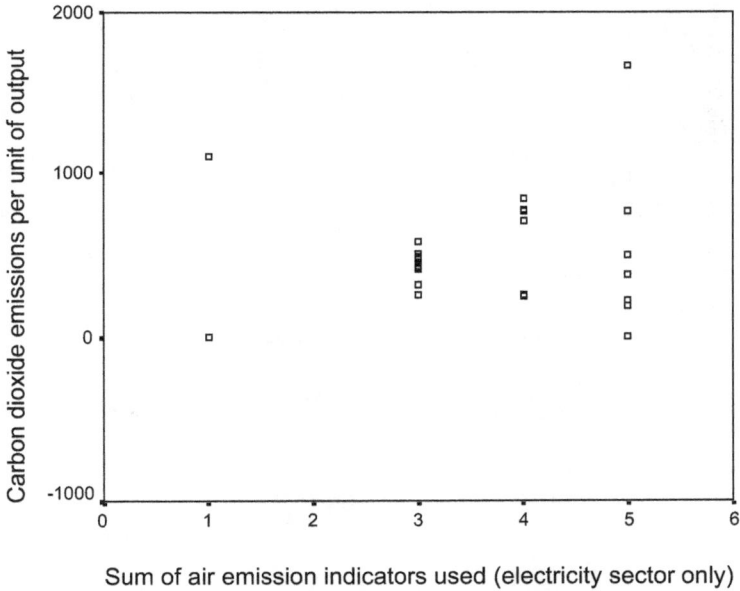

Figure I.1: Scatterplot for carbon dioxide emissions and five air emission indicators

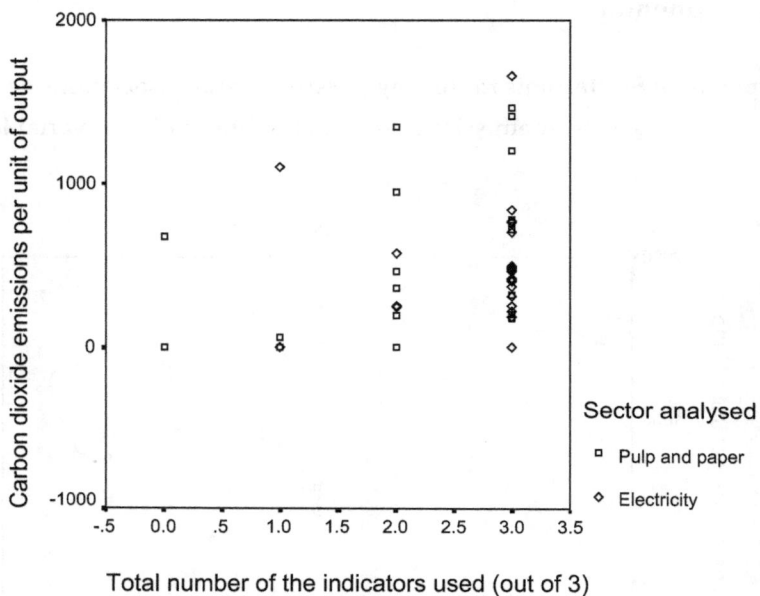

Figure I.2: Scatterplot for carbon dioxide emissions and three air emission indicators

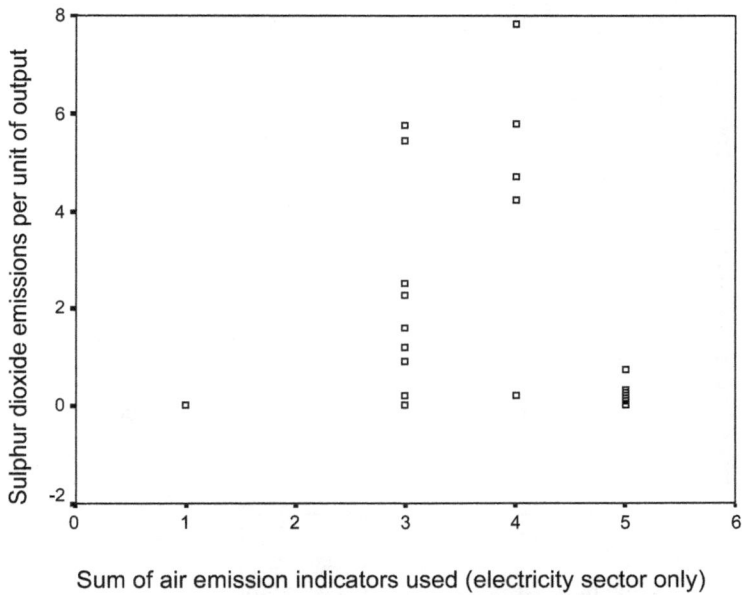

Figure I.3: Scatterplot for sulphur dioxide emissions and five air emission indicators

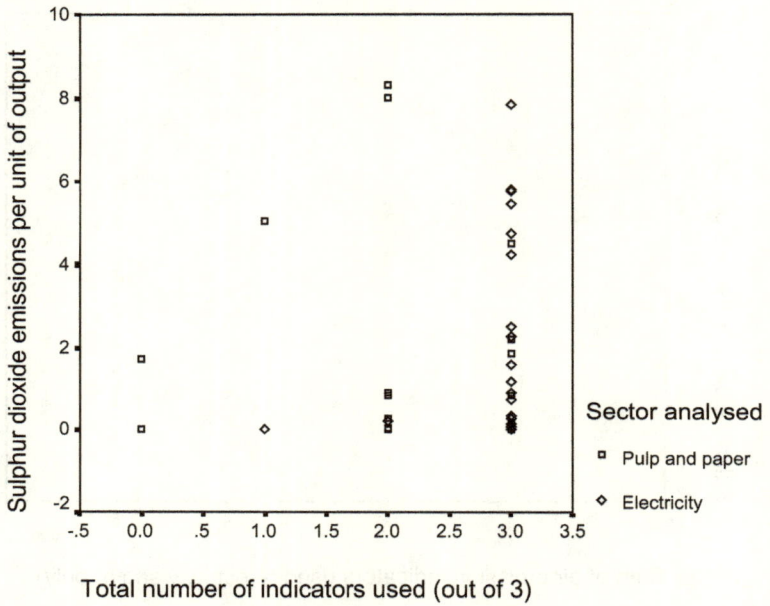

Figure I.4: Scatterplot for sulphur dioxide emissions and three air emission indicators

170

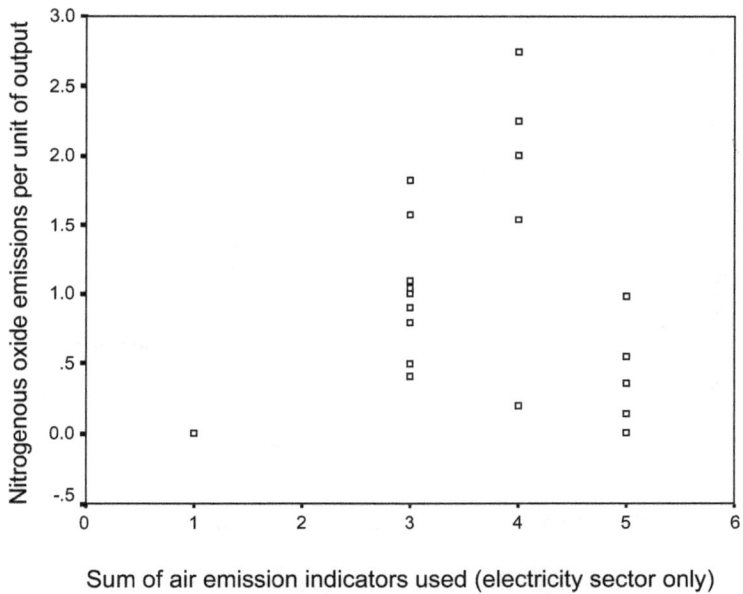

Figure I.5: Scatterplot for nitrogenous oxide emissions and five air
emission indicators

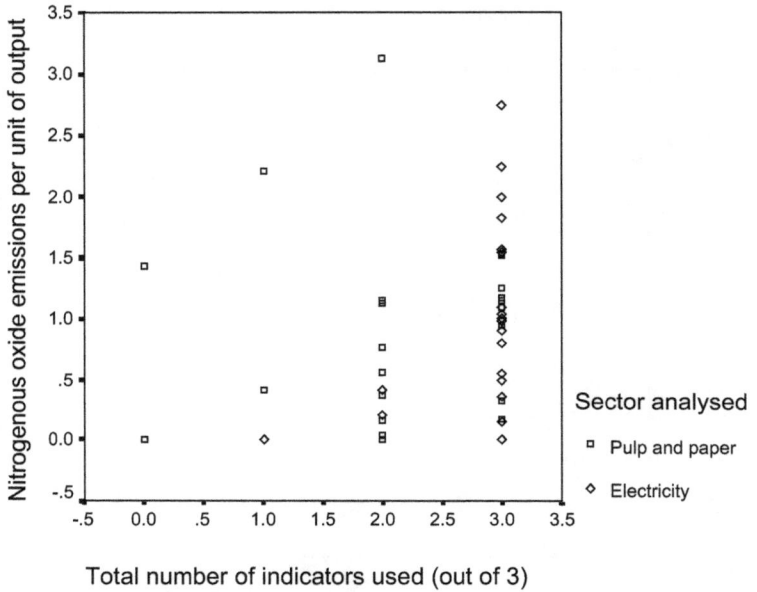

Figure I.6:   Scatterplot for nitrogenous oxide emissions and three air
emission indicators

Appendix II: Scatterplots for testing possible linear associations between water emissions variables and water emission indicator variables

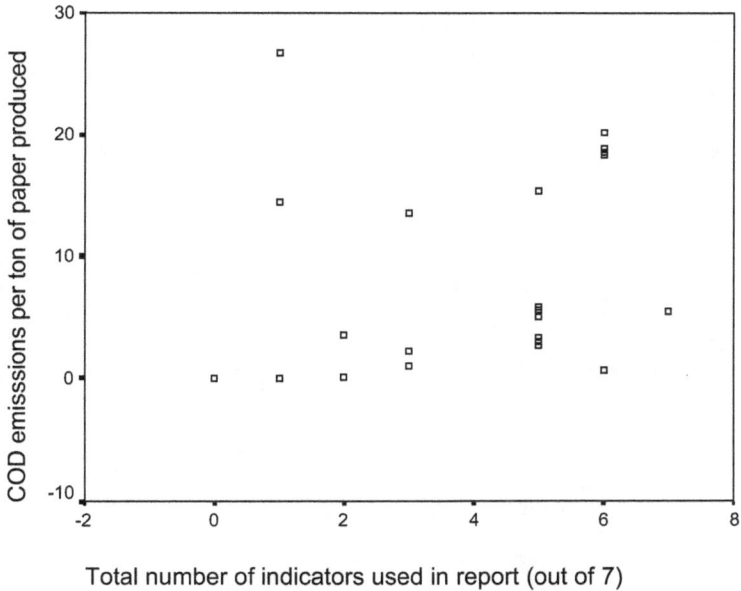

Figure II.1: Scatterplot for COD emissions and seven water emission
indicators

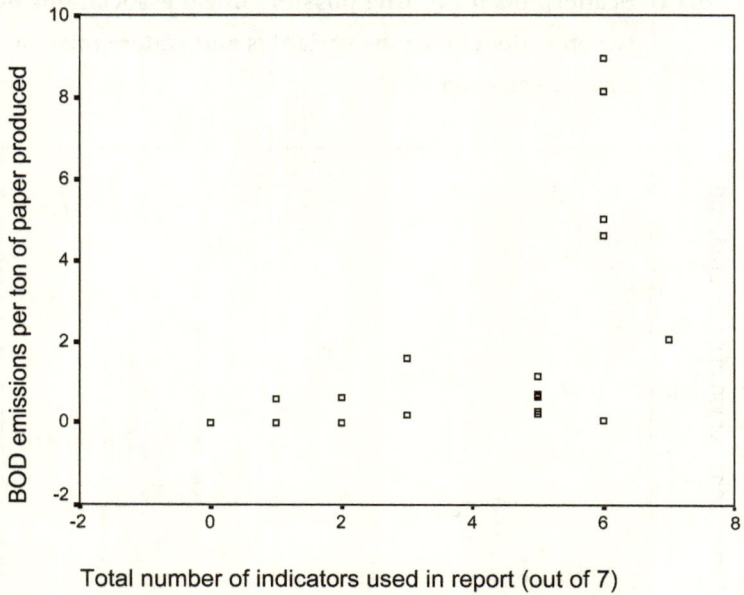

Figure II.2: Scatterplot for BOD emissions and seven water emission
indicators

174

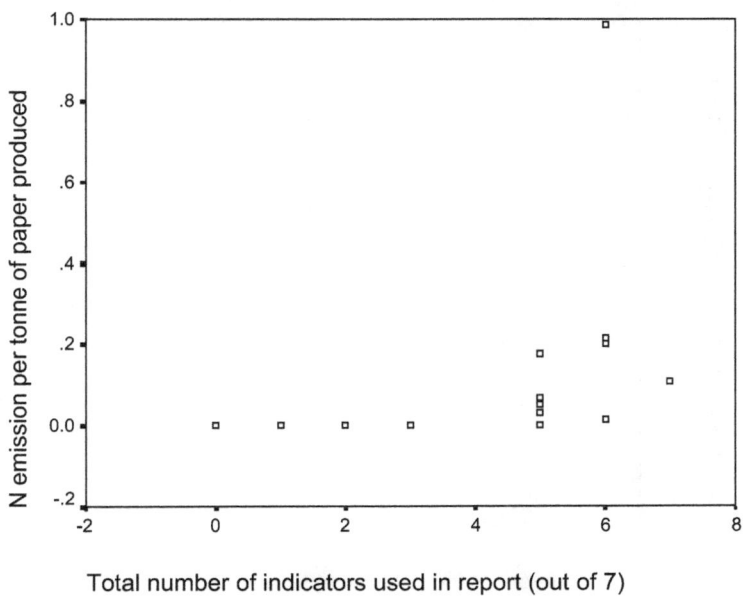

Figure II.3: Scatterplot for nitrogen emissions and seven water emission indicators

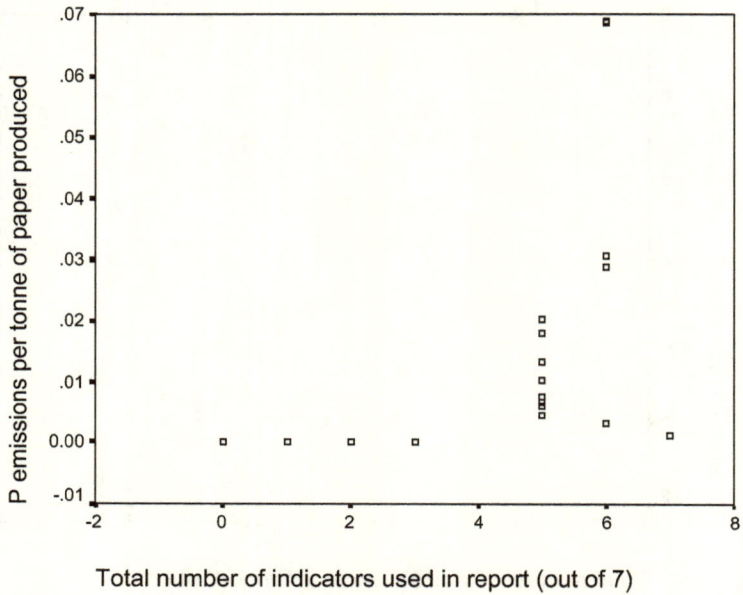

Figure II.4:   Scatterplot for phosphorous emissions and seven water
emission indicators

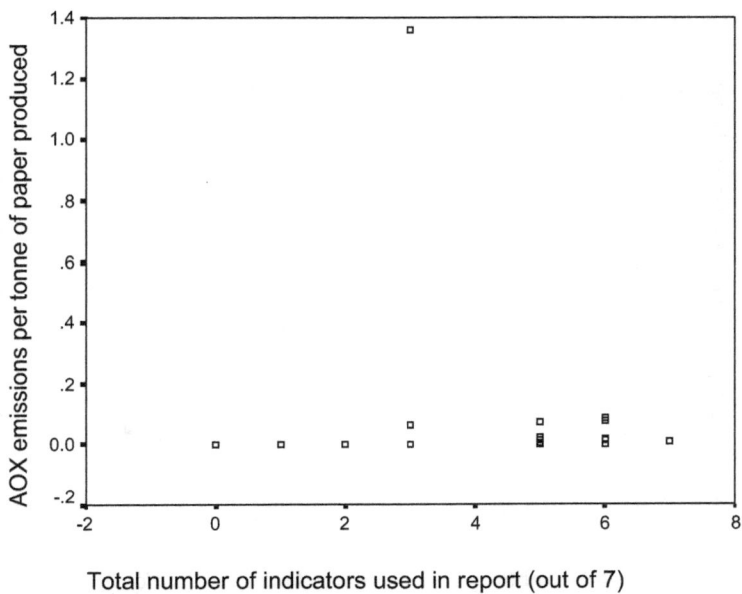

Figure II.5:   Scatterplot for AOX emissions and seven water emission
indicators

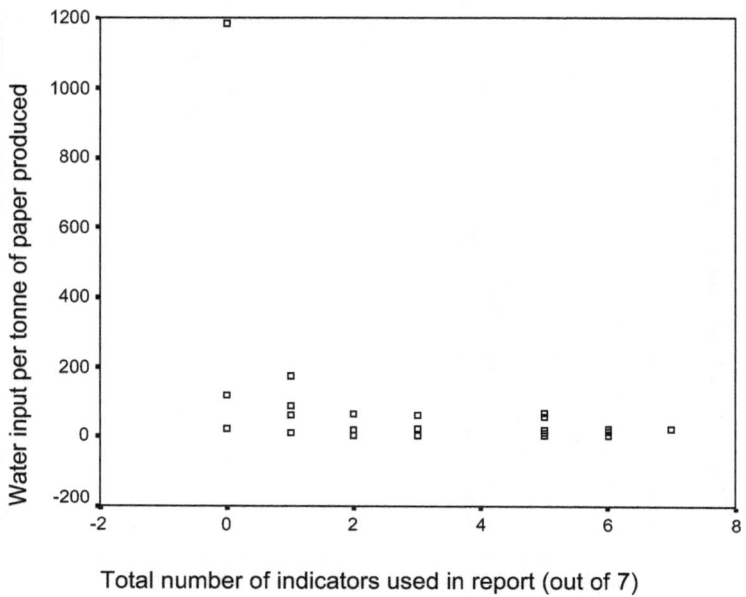

Figure II.6:   Scatterplot for water input and seven water emission
indicators

Appendix III: Scatterplots for testing possible linear associations between sum-of-indicators variables for water emissions
and the air emissions levels

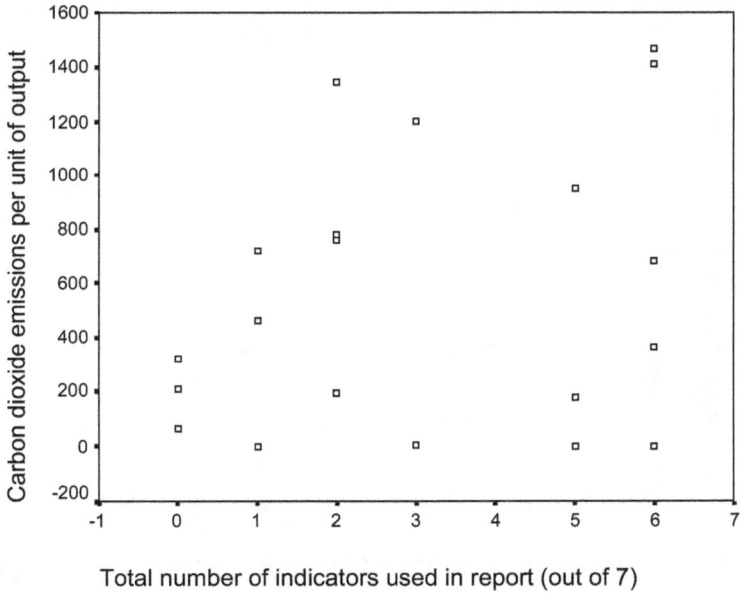

Figure III.1: Scatterplot for carbon dioxide emissions and 7 water emission indicators

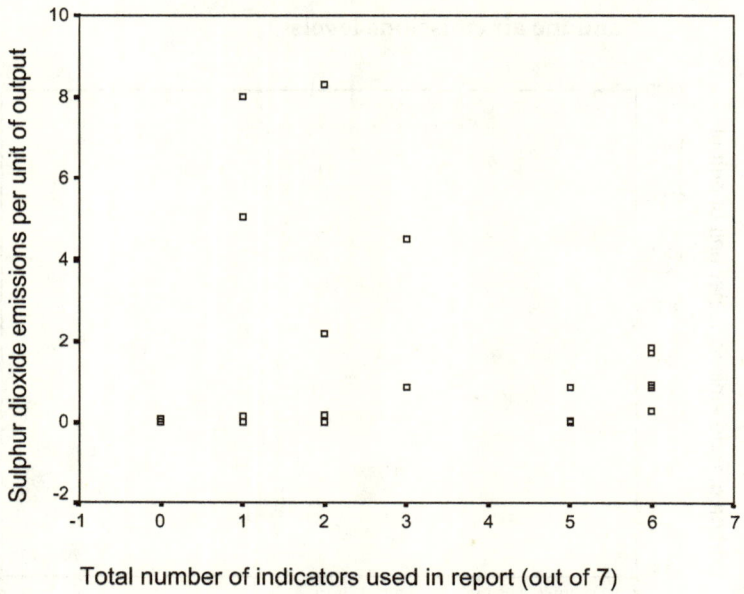

Figure III.2: Scatterplot for sulphur dioxide emissions and 7 water emission indicators

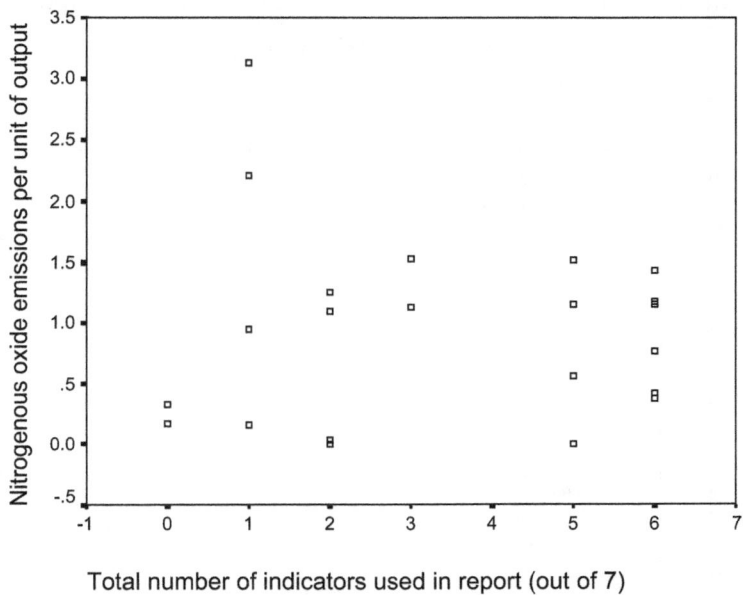

Figure III.3: Scatterplot for nitrogenous oxide emissions and 7 water
emission indicators

Appendix IV: Scatterplots for testing possible linear associations between sum-of-indicators variables for water and air emissions

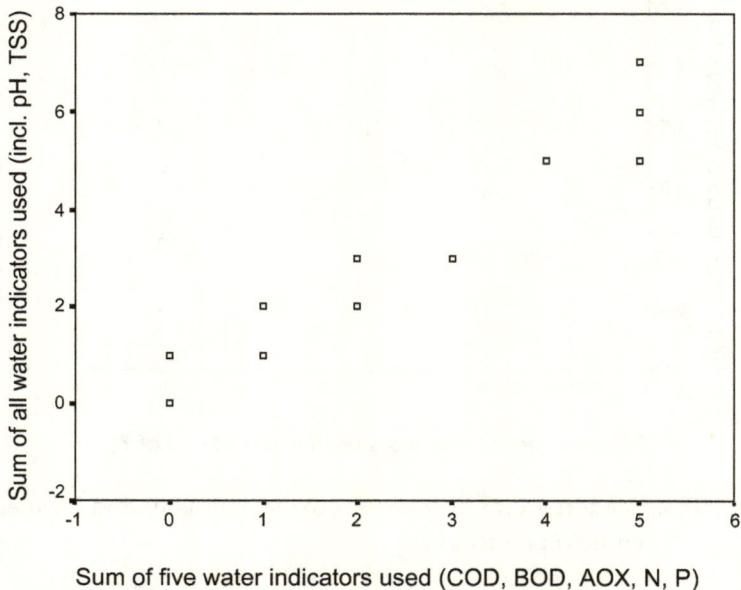

Figure IV.1: Scatterplot for the sum of five and seven water emission indicator variables

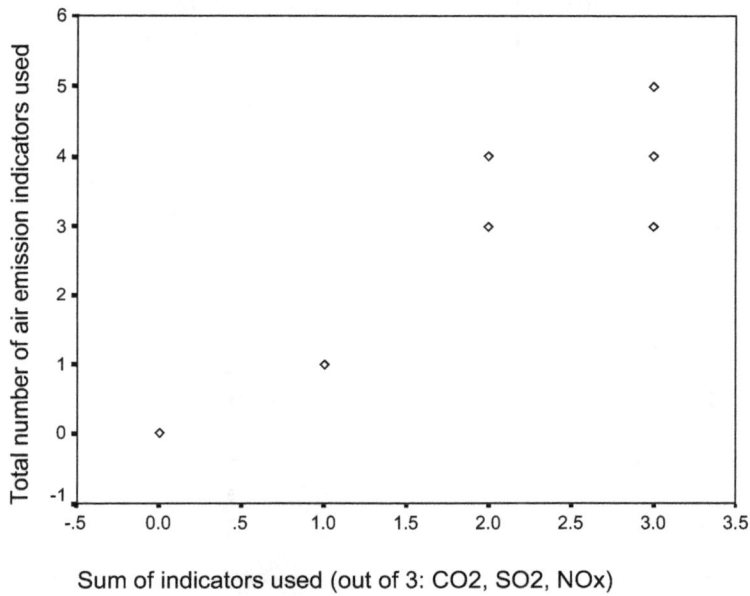

Figure IV.2: Scatterplot for the sum of three and five air emission
indicator variables

Appendix V: Scatterplots for visualising possible linear associations of factor scores and sum indicator variables for air and water emissions

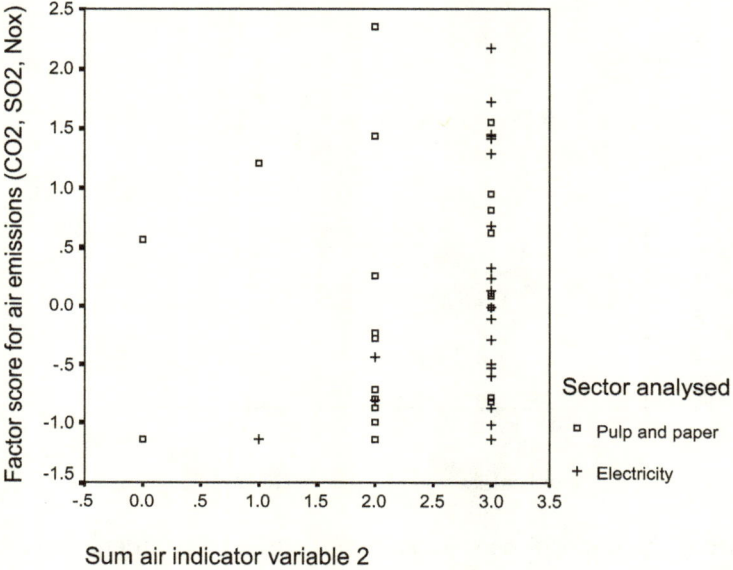

Figure V.1: Scatterplot for air emission factor score and sum air indicator variable 2 (different markers for both sectors)

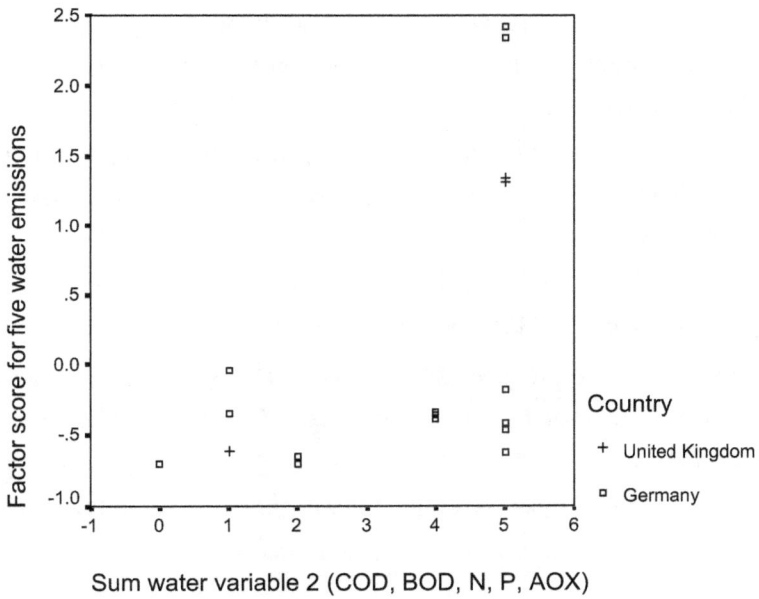

Figure V.2: Scatterplot for water emission factor score and sum water variable of BOD, COD, P, N and AOX emission indicators use (different markers for both countries)

List of References and Literature

Azzone, G., Noci, G., Manzini, R., Welford, R. & Young, W. (1996). Defining Environmental Performance Indicators. An Integrated Framework. *Business Strategy and the Environment*, 5(1), 69 - 80.

Azzone, G., Brophy, M., Noci, G., Welford, R. & Young, W. (1997). A Stakeholders' View of Environmental Reporting. *Long Range Planning*, 30(5), 699-709.

Bartolomeo, M. (1995). *Environmental Performance Indicators in Industry*. Milan: Fondazione Eni Enrico Mattei (FEEM).

Behmanesh, N., Roque, J. A. & Allen, D. T. (1993). An Analysis of Normalized Measures of Pollution Prevention. *Pollution Prevention Review*, Spring, 161-166.

Belzer, P. (2000). Written personal communication provided by Ms. Petra Belzer, Sales Manager, Bureau van Dijk. Frankfurt, 31st October 2000.

Bennett, M. & James, P. (1997). *Environment-Related Performance Measurement: Current Practice and Trends*. Ashridge: Ashridge Management College.

Bennett, M. & James, P. (1998). *Environment under the Spotlight - Current Practice and Future Trends in Environment-Related Performance Measurement for Business*. London: Association of Chartered Certified Accountants (ACCA).

Berkhout, F., Hertin, J., Tyteca, D., Carlens, J., Olsthoorn, X., van Druinen, M., van der Woerd, F., Azzone, G., Noci, G., Jasch, C., Wehrmeyer, W., Wagner, M., Gameson, T., Wolf, O. & Eames, M. (2001). *MEPI - Measuring Environmental Performance of Industry* (Final report and appendices submitted to the European Commission DG XII). Brussels European Commission.

BMWi (2001). *Nachhaltige Energiepolitik für eine zukunftsfähige Energieversorgung* (Sustainable energy policy for sustainable energy supply). Berlin: Bundeswirtschaftsministerium.

Brophy, M. & Starkey, R. (1996). Environmental Reporting. In: Welford, R. (ed.) *Corporate Environmental Management - Systems and Strategies.* London: Earthscan, 150-176.

Bundesamt für Umwelt (1991). *Ökobilanz von Packstoffen* (SRU Nr. 132, Aktualisierung '91). Bern: BUWAL.

Cable, J. (1984). *Employee Participation and Firm Performance: A Prisoners' Dilemma Framework* (EUI Working Paper 84/126). Florence: European University Institute.

Callens, I., & Tyteca, D. (1999). Towards indicators of sustainable development for firms - Concepts and definitions. *Ecological Economics, 28,* 41-53.

CEC (Commission of the European Communities) (1993). Council Regulation No. 1836/93 of June 1993 Allowing Voluntary Participation by Companies in the Industrial Sector in a Community Eco-Management and Audit Scheme. *Official Journal of the European Communities,* L168, 1-18.

CEC (Commission of the European Communities) (2001). Corrigendum to Regulation (EC) No. 761/2001 of the European Parliament and of the Council fo 19 March 2001 Allowing Voluntary Participation by Organisations in a Community Eco-Management and Audit Scheme (EMAS). *Official Journal of the European Communities,* L114, 24 April 2001.

CEFIC (European Chemical Industry Council) (1998). *Responsible Care - Health Safety and Environmental Reporting Guidelines*. Brussels: CEFIC.

CERES (Coalition for Environmentally Responsible Economies) (1998). Global Reporting Initiative (GRI) web page. URL: http://www.ceres.org/ reporting/globalreporting.html, accessed 21 September 1998.

Charter, M. (1998). Electronic environmental reporting. *Environmental Accounting & Auditing Reporter*, 3(8), 2-3.

CICA (1994). *Reporting on Environmental Performance*. Toronto (Canada): Canadian Institute of Chartered Accountants.

Clausen, J. & Klaffke, K. (2000). Kommunizieren oder Erbsen zählen (To communicate or to count peas). *Ökologisches Wirtschaften*, 5/2000, 4.

Confederation of the European Paper Industry (CEPI) (1998). *CEPI Annual Statistics 1997*. Brussels: Confederation of the European Paper Industry.

Cowell, S. J. (1998). *Environmental Life Cycle Assessment of Agricultural Systems: Integration into Decision-Making* (PhD thesis). Guildford: Centre for Environmental Strategy, University of Surrey.

Dalal-Clayton, B., Bass, S., Sadler, B., Thomson, K., Sandbrook, R., Robins, N., & Hughes, R. (1994). National Sustainable Development Strategies: Experience and Dilemmas. *Environmental Planning Issues*, No. 6.

DeSimone, L. & Popoff, F. (1997). *Eco-Efficiency: The Business Link to Sustainable Development*. Cambridge: MIT Press.

DIN (1995). *Umweltmanagementsysteme - Spezifikationen und Leitlinien zur Anwendung (ISO/DIS 14001)*. Berlin: Deutsches Institut für Normung (DIN).

Ditz, D. & Ranganathan, J. (1997). *Measuring Up. Towards a Common Framework for Tracking Corporate Environmental Performance.* Washington D.C.: World Resources Institute (WRI).

Edwards, D. (1998). *The Link between Company Environmental and Financial Performance.* London: Earthscan.

Elkington, J., Kreander, N., & Stibbard, H. (1998). The Third International Survery on Company Environmental Reporting: The 1997 Benchmark Survey. *Greener Management International,* 21, 99-111.

Endres, A. (1994). *Umweltökonomie (Environmental Economics).* Darmstadt: Wissenschaftliche Buchgesellschaft.

ENDS (2000) Firms get sustainability reporting guidance, *ENDS Environment Daily,* 30/06/00, http://www.ends.co.uk/envdaily, accessed 30/06/00.

European Community (EC) (1993). *EU Regulation (EEC) No 1836/93 of 29 June 1993 Allowing Voluntary Participation by Companies in the Industrial Sector in a Community Eco-Management and Audit Scheme.* Brussels: European Community.

Fava, J., Jensen, A. *et al.* (1992). *Life-Cycle Assessment Data Quality. A Conceptual Framework.* Wintergreen: SETAC.

Federal Environment Ministry (BMU) & Federal Environmental Agency (UBA) (1997). *A Guide to Corporate Environmental Indicators.* Bonn and Berlin: Federal Environment Ministry (BMU) and Federal Environmental Agency (UBA).

Freedman, M., & Jaggi, B. (1988). Impact of Government Regulations on Pollution Performance of Pulp and Paper Firms. *Environmental Management,* 12(3), 391-396.

future e.V. & IÖW (ed.) (1998). *Umweltberichte und Umwelterklärungen: Ranking 1998. Zusammenfassung der Ergebnisse und Trends* (Environmental reports and environmental statements: ranking 1998: summary of results and trends). Munich: future e.V.

Gee, D., & Moll, D. (1998). *Information for Sustainability: Eco-Efficiency Indicators*. Copenhagen: European Environment Agency (EEA).

Gijtenberg, M., Piet, J., & White A. L. (1996). The Greening of Corporate Accounting. In: P. Groenewegen P., Fischer, K., Jenkins, E. & Schot, J. E. (eds.) *The Greening of Industry Resource Guide and Bibliography*. Washington: Island Press, 137-168.

Gilbert, M. (1994). BS7750 and the Eco-Management and Audit Regulation. *Eco-Management and Auditing*, 1(2), 6-10.

Grafe-Buckens A. (1997). *The EMAS Environmental Statement - Final Report to the European Commission*. Brussels: EC DG XI.

Grafe-Buckens, A. (1998). Environmental Statements: Meeting the User's Needs. Paper presented at the International Institute of Industrial Environmental Economics (IIIEE) Invitational Seminar "Continuity, Credibility and Comparability", 13-16 June, Eze, France.

Gravetter, F. J. & Wallnau, L. B. (1996). *Statistics for the Behavioural Sciences: A First Course for Students of Psychology and Education* (4th ed.). St. Paul: West.

Gobbo, F. (1981). The Pulp and Paper Industry: Structure and Behaviour. In: De Jong, H. W. (ed.) *The Structure of European Industry*, Martinus Nijhoff Publishers, 57-91.

Gordon, J. (1994). Environmental Policy in Britain and Germany: Some Comparisons. *European Environment*, 4(3), 9-12.

Graichen, P. (2002). Energiepolitik als Ausdruck umweltpolitischer Konflikte: Ein historischer Rückblick auf die Umwelt- und Energiepolitik in Deutschland (Energy policy as an expression of conflicts in environmental policy: a historical review of environmental and energy policy in Germany). *Zeitschrift für Energiewirtschaft*, 26(3), 209-218.

GRI (Global Reporting Initiative) (2002). *Sustainability Reporting Guidelines*. Boston: GRI.

GRI (2000). http://www.globalreporting.org/Guidelines/June2000/June2000GuidelinesDownload.htm, accessed 19 January 2001.

GRI (2000b). http://globalreporting.org/Guidelines/June2000/Supporting-Documents/FacilityLinking.htm, accessed 19 January 2001.

Guinée, J. & R. Heijungs (1993). A Proposal for the Classification of Toxic Substances within the Framework of Life-Cycle Assessment of Products. *Chemosphere*, 26(10), 1925-1944.

Handler, T. (1997). Environmental Regulation in England and Wales. In: Handler, T. (ed.) *Regulating the European Environment* (2nd ed.). John Wiley: Chichester & New York, 55-73.

Hart, S. L. and Ahuja, G. (1996). Does it Pay to be Green? An Empirical Examination of the Relationship between Emission Reduction and Firm Performance. *Business Strategy and the Environment*, 5, 30-37.

Hay, D. A. & Morris, D. J. (1991). *Industrial Economics & Organization: Theory & Evidence* (2nd ed.). Oxford: Oxford University Press.

Heijungs, R., Guinée, J., Huppes, G., Lankreijer, R. H., Udo de Haes, H. & Sleeswijk, A. (1992). *Environmental Life Cycle Assessment of Products: Guide and Backgrounds*. Leiden: CML.

Hill, C. & Jones, G. (1992). *Strategic Management. An Integrated Approach*. Boston: Houghton Mifflin.

Hofstetter, P. & Heijungs, R. (1996). Definitions of terms and symbols, In: Udo de Haes, H. (ed.) *Towards a Methodology for Life Cycle Impact Assessment.* Brussels: SETAC Europe, 31-39.

Hunt, D., & Johnson, C. (1992). *Environmental Management Systems: Principals and Practice.* London: McGraw Hill.

ICI (1997). *Environmental Burden: The ICI Approach.* London: ICI.

IMUG, IÖW, IFEU, Öko-Institut (2000). *German Environmental Institutes' Common Statement of Position on the GRI Sustainability Reporting Guidelines.* Hannover: IMUG, November 2000.

IRRC (Investor Responsibility Research Centre) (1995). *Environmental Reporting and Third Party Statements.* Washington, DC: Investor Responsibility Research Centre (IRRC) and Global Environmental Management Institute.

ISO (International Standards Organisation) (1996). *International Standard ISO 14031 Environmental Management - Environmental Performance Evaluation.* Geneva: ISO.

ISO (International Standards Organisation) (1997). *International Standard ISO 14040 Environmental Management - Life Cycle Assessment - Principles and Framework.* Geneva: ISO.

ISO (International Standards Organisation) (1999). *ISO 14031 Environmental Management - Environmental Performance Evaluation - Guidelines.* Geneva: ISO.

Jaggi, B. & Freedman, M. (1992). An Examination of the Impact of Pollution Performance on Economic and Market Performance of Pulp and Paper Firms. *Journal of Business Finance & Accounting,* 19.5, 697-713.

James, P., & Bennett, M. (1996). *Environment-related Performance Measurement in Business - From Emissions to Profit and Sustainability?* Ashridge: Ashridge Management Research Group.

James, P. & Wehrmeyer, W. (1996). Environmental Performance Measurement. In: Groenewegen, P., Fischer, K., Jenkins, E. G. & Schot J. E. (eds.) *The Greening of Industry Resource Guide and Bibliography.* Washington: Island Press, 111-136.

Johnson, S. D. (1996). Environmental Performance Evaluation: Prioritizing Environmental Performance Objectives. *Corporate Environmental Strategy,* Autumn, 17-28.

Johnston, J. & DiNardo, J. (1997). *Econometric Methods* (4th ed.). New York: McGraw-Hill.

Kinnear, P. R. & Gray, C. D. (1997). *SPSS for Windows Made Simple* (2nd ed.). Howe: Psychology Press.

Keffer, C., Shimp, R. & Lehni, M. (1999). *Eco-Efficiency Indicators & Reporting – Report on the Status of the Project's Work in Progress and Guideline for Pilot Application.* Geneva: WBCSD, April 1999.

Kohler, U. & Kreuter, F. (2001). *Datenanalyse mit Stata: allgemeine Konzepte der Datenanalyse und ihre praktische Anwendung* (Data analysis with Stata: general concepts of data analysis and their practical application). Munich: Oldenbourg.

KPMG (1996). *The KPMG UK Environmental Reporting Survey 1996.* London: KPMG.

Lascelles, D. (1993). *Rating Environmental Risk.* London: Center for the Study of Financial Innovation.

Ledgerwood, G., Street, E., & Therivel, R. (1993). *The Environmental Audit and Business Strategy - A Total Quality Approach.* London: Pitman.

Lehni, M. (1998). *Eco-Metrics must be Eco-Efficiency Metrics*. WBCDS Workshop, Antwerp.

Leipert, C. (1989). *Die Heimlichen Kosten des Fortschritts - Wie Umweltzerstörung das Wirtschaftswachstum fördert*. Frankfurt/Main: S. Fischer.

Loew, T., & Kottmann, H. (1996). Kennzahlen im Umweltmanagement. *Ökologisches Wirtschaften*, 1, 10-12.

May, P. H., & de Motta, R. S. (1996). *Pricing the Planet - Economic Analysis of Sustainable Development*. New York: Columbia University Press.

Müller, K., de Frutos, J. *et al.* (1994). *Environmental Reporting and Disclosures. The Financial Analysts View*. London: Workings Group of Environmental Issues of the Accounting Commission of the European Federation of Financial Analysts Society (EFFAS).

Müller-Wenk, R. (1978). *Die Ökologische Buchhaltung. Ein Informations- und Steuerungsinstrument für umweltkonforme Unternehmenspolitik* (Ecological book-keeping. An information and decision-support instrument for environmentally sensitive corporate policy). Frankfurt/Main: Campus Verlag.

NRTEE (National Roundtable on the Environment and the Economy) (1997). *Backgrounder: Measuring Eco-efficiency in Business*. Ottawa, Canada: National Roundtable on the Environment and the Economy.

Neely, A. (1993). *Performance Measurement System Design - A Process-based Approach*. Cambridge: University of Cambridge, Manufacturing Engineering Group.

Olsthoorn, X., Tyteca, D., Wehrmeyer, W. & Wagner, M. (2001). Using Environmental Indicators for Business - A Literature Review and the Need for Standardisation and Aggregation of Data. *Journal of Cleaner Production*, 9(5), 453-463.

Pearce, D. W. & Turner, R. K. (1990). *Economics of Resources and the Environment*. Hemel Hempstead, Hertfordshire: Harvester Wheatsheaf .

Porter, M. (1991) America's Green Strategy. *Scientific American*, 264(4), 96.

Rubik, F. & Baumgartner, T. (1992). *Technological Innovation in the Plastics Industry and its Influence on the Environmental Problems of Plastic Waste: Evaluation of Eco-Balances* (MONITOR: Strategic Analysis in Science & Technology (SAST) Activity, Project 7). Brussels: Commission of the European Communities.

Rudestam, K. E. & Newton, R. R. (1992). *Surviving your Thesis: A Comprehensive Guide to Content and Process*. Newbury Park, CA: Sage.

Russo, M. V. & Fouts, P. A. (1997). A Resource-Based Perspective on Corporate Environmental Performance and Profitability. *Academy of Management Journal*, 40, 534-559.

Schaltegger, S. (1996). Life Cycle Assessment (LCA). Quo Vadis? Basel: Birkhäuser.

Schaltegger, S. (1997). Economics of Life Cycle Assesment: Inefficiency of the present approach. *Business Strategy and the Environment*, 6, 1-8.

Schaltegger, S. & Burritt, R. (2000). *Contemporary Environmental Accounting*. Sheffield: Greenleaf.

Schaltegger, S. & Figge, F. (1998). *Environmental Shareholder Value* (Sarasin Basic Report Nr. 54). Basel: Bank Sarasin/Center of Economics and Business Administration, Basel University.

Schaltegger, S. & Figge, F. (2000). Environmental shareholder value: economic success with corporate environmental management. *Eco-Management and Auditing*, 7(1), 29-42.

Schaltegger, S. & R. Kubat (1995). *Glossary of LCA. Terms and Definitions* (WWZ-Study No. 45). Basel: Basel University.

Schaltegger, S. & Sturm, A. (1992). *Ökologieorientierte Entscheidungen in Unternehmen. Ökologisches Rechnungswesen statt Ökobilanzierung: Notwendigkeit, Kriterien, Konzepte* (Environmentally Oriented Decisions in Companies. Environmental Accounting instead of Eco-balancing: Necessity, Criteria, Concepts) (1st ed.). Bern: Haupt.

Schaltegger, S. & Sturm, A. (1994). *Ökologieorientierte Entscheidungen in Unternehmen. Ökologisches Rechnungswesen statt Ökobilanzierung: Notwendigkeit, Kriterien, Konzepte* (2nd ed.). Bern: Haupt.

Schaltegger, S. & Sturm, A. (1996). Managerial Eco-Control in Manufacturing and Process Industries. *Greener Management International*, 13, 78-91.

Schaltegger, S. & Synnestvedt, T. (2002). The Link Between „Green" and Economic Success. Environmental Management as the Crucial Trigger between Environmental and Economic Performance. *Journal of Environmental Management*, 65, 339-346.

Schaltegger, S., Burritt, R. & Petersen, H. (2003). *An Introduction to Corporate Environmental Management*. Sheffield: Greenleaf Publishing.

Schmidheiny, S. & BCSD (Business Council for Sustainable Development) (1992). *Changing Course: A Global Business Perspective on Development and the Environment*. Palatino and Cambridge, Mass.: MIT Press.

Schmidheiny, S., & Zorraquin, F. J. L. (1996). *Financing Change: The Financial Community, Eco-Efficiency and Sustainable Development*. Cambridge, Mass.: MIT Press.

Scherer, J. (1997). Environmental Regulation in the Federal Republic of Germany In Handler,T (ed.) *Regulating the European Environment* (2nd ed.). Chichester & New York: John Wiley, pp. 89-112.

Schreiner, M. (1991). *Umweltmanagement in 22 Lektionen. Ein ökonomischer Weg in einer ökologische Gesellschaft* (Environmental management in 22 lessons: an economical way towards an ecological society). Wiesbaden: Gabler Verlag.

Schulz, E., & Schulz, W. (1993). *Umweltcontrolling in der Praxis*. Munich: Verlag Vahlen.

Seidel, E. (1988). Ökologisches Controlling (Ecological controlling). In: Wunderer, R. (ed.) *Betriebswirtschaftslehre als Management- und Führungslehre* (Business administration theory as a theory of management and leadership) (2nd ed.). Stuttgart: C.E. Poeschel Verlag, 301-322.

Seidel, E. (1992) Entwicklung eines betrieblich-ökologischen Rechnungswesens. Schlüssel zu einer tatsächlichen Ökologisierung des Wirtschaftens. In: Seidel, E. (ed.) *Betrieblicher Umweltschutz. Landschaftsökologie und Betriebswirtschaftslehre*. Wiesbaden, 229-246.

SETAC (Society of Environmental Toxicology and Chemistry - Europe) (1992). *Life-cycle Assessment*. Brussels: SETAC-Europe.

Skillius, A. & Wennberg, U. (1998). *Continuity, Credibility and Comparability: Key Challenges for Corporate Environmental Performance Measurement and Communication*. Lund, Sweden: IIIEE, Lund University.

Smith, A. (1998). *Environmental Aspects of the Pulp and Paper Industry. Background Paper for the Research Project "Measuring Environmental Performance in Industry"*. Brighton: Science Policy Research Unit (SPRU), University of Sussex.

Spiller, A. (1996). *Ökologieorientierte Produktpolitik*. Marburg: Metropolis.

197

StataCorp (1997). *Stata Statistical Software: Release 5.0*. Stata Corp., College Station, TX.

Technical Committee 207 (1996). *International Standard ISO14031 Environmental Management - Environmental Performance Evaluation*. Geneva: International Standards Organisation.

Tennant, T., Belsom, T. & Thomas, C. (1997). *Creating a Standard for a Corporate Global Warming Indicator*. London: National Provident Investment (NPI).

Tyteca, D. (1996). On the Measurement of the Environmental Performance of Firms – A Literature Review and a Productive Efficiency Perspective. *Journal of Environmental Management*, 46, 281-308.

Tyteca, D. (1997). *On Sustainability Indicators at the Firm Level: Pollution and Resource Efficiency as a Necessary Condition towards Sustainability*. Louvain-la-Neuve: Université Catholique de Louvain-la-Neuve (UCL).

Tyteca, D. (1999). Sustainability indicators at the firm level - Pollution and resource efficiency as a necessary condition towards sustainability. *Journal of Industrial Ecology*, 2(4), 183-197.

Tyteca, D., Carlens, J., Berkhout, F., Hertin, J., Wehrmeyer, W. and Wagner, M. (2002). Corporate Environmental Performance Evaluation: Evidence from the MEPI Project. *Business Strategy and the Environment*, 11, 1-13.

Udo de Haes, H. (1995). *The Methodology of Life Cycle Impact Assessment. Report of the SETAC-Europe Working Groups on Life Cycle Impact Assessment*. Leiden: CML.

Udo de Haes, H. (1996). *Towards a Methodology for Life Cycle Impact Assessment*. Brussels: SETAC-Europe.

UNEP (United Nations Environment Programme) & SustainAbility (1996). *Engaging Stakeholders Volume 1: The Benchmark Survey.* Paris/London: UNEP/Sustainability.

UNEP & SustainAbility (1997). *Engaging Stakeholders, The 1997 Benchmark Survey.* Paris/London: UNEP/Sustainability.

UNEP & Sustainability (1998). *Engaging Stakeholders 1998: The CEO Agenda.* London: SustainAbility.

Wackernagel M. & Rees W. (1996). *Our Ecological Footprint - Reducing Human Impact on the Earth.* Gabriola Island: New Society.

Wagner, J. (1998). Bestimmungsgründe internationaler Firmentätigkeit – Ergebnisse ökonometrischer Untersuchungen mit Daten aus niedersächsischen Industriebetrieben (Determinants of international firm activities – results of econometric analyses with data from industrial entreprises in Lower Saxony). *Jahrbücher für Nationalökonomie und Statistik,* 217, 613-627.

Wagner, M. (2000). The Relationship between Environmental and Economic Performance of Firms. Paper presented at the 2nd POSTI meeting in collaboration with the ESST Annual Scientific Conference, Strasbourg, 27-28 May, http://www.esst.uio.no/posti/workshops/wagner.html

Wagner, M. (2003a). *How Does it Pay to Be Green? An Analysis of the Relationship between Environmental and Economic Performance at the Firm Level and the Influence of Corporate Environmental Strategy Choice.* Marburg: Tectum.

Wagner, M. (2003b). Does it Pay to Be Eco-Efficient in the European Electricity Supply Industry? *Zeitschrift für Energiewirtschaft,* 27, 309-319.

Wagner, M. (2004). Sustainable Reporting? The Link of Environmental Reports and Environmental Performance. *Corporate Environmental Strategy – International Journal for Sustainable Business,* 11, Nov-Dec, 4-21.

Wagner, M. (2005a). Sustainability and Competitive Advantage: Empirical Evidence on the Influence of Strategic Choices between Environmental Management Approaches. *Environmental Quality Management,* forthcoming.

Wagner, M. (2005b). A Panel Data Analysis on Sustainability Strategies in the European Paper Industry: Environmental and Economic Performance reconciled? *Journal of Environmental Management,* forthcoming.

Wagner, M. (2005c). Environmental Performance and the Quality of Corporate Environmental Reports: The Role of Environmental Management Accounting. In: Rikhardsson, P., Bennett, M., Schaltegger S., Bouma, J.J. (eds.) *Implementing Environmental Management Accounting: Status and Challenges.* Dordrecht: Kluwer Academic Publishers, 45-62.

Wagner, M. & Schaltegger, S. (2004a). How Does Sustainability Performance Relate to Business Competitiveness? *Greener Management International,* 44, 5-16.

Wagner, M. & Schaltegger, S. (2004b). The Effect of Corporate Environmental Strategy Choice and Environmental Performance on Competitiveness and Economic Performance: An Empirical Analysis of EU Manufacturing. *European Management Journal,* 22(5), 557-572.

Wagner, M., Nguyen Van, P., Azomahou, T. & Wehrmeyer, W. (2002). The Relationship between the Environmental and Economic Performance of Firms: An Empirical Analysis of the European Paper Industry. *Corporate Social Responsibility and Environmental Management,* 9, 133-146.

Wallace, A. & Parker, W. (1996). Measuring and Reporting Environmental Performance in a Global Company: A Case for Material Accounting. Communication to the Fifth International Research Conference of the Greening of Industry Network, Heidelberg.

WBCSD (World Business Council for Sustainable Development) (1998). *Eco-efficiency Metrics and Reporting (Eco-efficiency Brief No. 1).* Geneva: WBCSD.

WBCSD (2000). *Measuring Eco-Efficiency - a guide to reporting company performance.* Geneva: World Business Council for Sustainable Development.

Wehrmeyer, W. (1993). *A Comparative Study of Management Styles and Environmental Performance in Paper Manufacturing Industries* (PhD thesis). Canterbury: University of Kent at Canterbury.

Wehrmeyer, W. (1995). *Measuring Environmental Business Performance: A Comprehensive Guide.* Business and the Environment - Practitioner Series, Stanley Thornes.

Wehrmeyer, W. (1998). Physical Environmental Performance Indicators. Paper presented at the International Institute of Industrial Environmental Economics (IIIEE) Invitational Seminar "Continuity, Credibility and Comparability", 13-16 June, Eze, France.

Wehrmeyer, W. (1998b). Oral communication of Dr Walter Wehrmeyer, BG Surrey Scholar, Centre for Environmental Strategy. University of Surrey, 6 December 1998.

Wehrmeyer, W. & Tyteca, D. (1998). Measuring Environmental Performance for Industry: From Legitimacy to Sustainability? *The International Journal of Sustainable Development and World Ecology,* 5, 111-124.

Wells, R., Hockman, M., Hochman, S. & O'Connell, P. (1992). Measuring Environmental Success. *Total Environmental Quality Management,* Summer, 315-327.

Wernick, I. K. & Ausubel, J. H. (1995). National Material Metrics for Industrial Ecology. *Resources Policy*, 321(3), 189-198.

Willig, T. (ed.) (1994). *Environmental TQM*. New York: McGraw Hill.

WICE (World Industry Council for the Environment) (1994). *Environmental Reporting - A Manager's Guide*. Paris: WICE.

Wright, M., Allen, D., Clift, R. & Sas, H. (1997). Measuring Corporate Environmental Performance: The ICI Environmental Burden System. *Journal of Industrial Ecology*, 1(4), 117-127.

Wolters, D. T. (2001). Towards Sustainability Indicators for Product Chains. Paper for the special workshop of the Environmental Management Accounting Network (EMAN). Ninth Conference of the Greening of Industry Network, Bangkok, January 2001.

Young, W. & Rikhardsson, P. M. (1996). From corporate environmental performance indicators to corporate sustainability indicators: an evolutionary approach. Communication to the Fifth International Research Conference of the Greening of Industry Network, Heidelberg.

Young, W. & Welford, R. (1998). Environmental Performance Management Framework for Business. *Greener Management International*, 21, 30-49.

Zavatta, R. (1993). The Pulp and Paper Industry. In: de Jong, H. W. (ed.) *The Structure of European Industry* (3rd rev. ed.). Dordrecht: Kluwer Academic Publishers, 91-119.

About the Author:

Marcus Wagner Dipl.-Volkswirt, MBA, Dr. rer. pol. is an Associate Research Fellow at the Centre for Sustainability Management (CSM) and a Visiting Lecturer and Habilitation Candidate at the University of Lüneburg. He also teaches microeconomic theory and the theory of growth, distribution and business cycles at Hagen University. Prior positions were at the Universities of Lüneburg and Cottbus, the Centre for Environmental Strategy (Guildford) and the Institute of Energy and Sustainable Development (Leicester). Current work focuses on sustainability management strategies, esp. corporate sustainability strategies in deregulated energy markets and empirical research on corporate sustainability management.

Marcus was also scientific advisor to the Global Reporting Initiative's Measurement Working Group and has worked and published widely on issues such as sustainability performance and competitiveness, environmental performance measurement, sustainability balanced scorecard and the influence of corporate environmental strategy choice on the relationship between environmental and economic performance.

His work appears in journals *such as Journal of Environmental Management, European Management Journal, European Environment, Corporate Social Responsibility and Environmental Management, Business Strategy and the Environment, Environmental Quality Management* and *European Business Forum.* Marcus is a reviewer for *Greener Management International,* the *Journal of Cleaner Production* and the *Journal of Environmental Management.*

Recent books include:

Wagner, M. (2003) *How Does it Pay to Be Green?* Marburg: Tectum.

www.ingramcontent.com/pod-product-compliance
Lightning Source LLC
Chambersburg PA
CBHW020833210326
41598CB00019B/1891